W9-CPB-321

Lake Zurich MS North
LIBRARY
95 Hubbard Lane
Hawthorn Woods, IL 60047

Lake Zurich MS North
LIBRARY
95 Hubbard Lane
Hawthorn Woods, IL 60047

COMPACT *Research*

Impulse
Control
Disorders

Diseases and Disorders

ReferencePoint
Press®

San Diego, CA

Other books in the Compact Research Diseases and Disorders set:

ADHD
Anxiety Disorders
Bipolar Disorders
Mood Disorders
Obsessive-Compulsive Disorders
Personality Disorders
Phobias
Post-Traumatic Stress Disorders

*For a complete list of titles please visit www.referencepointpress.com.

Impulse Control Disorders

Peggy J. Parks

Diseases and Disorders

ReferencePoint
Press®

San Diego, CA

© 2013 ReferencePoint Press, Inc.
Printed in the United States

For more information, contact:
ReferencePoint Press, Inc.
PO Box 27779
San Diego, CA 92198
www.ReferencePointPress.com

ALL RIGHTS RESERVED.
No part of this work covered by the copyright hereon may be reproduced or used in any form or by any means—graphic, electronic, or mechanical, including photocopying, recording, taping, web distribution, or information storage retrieval systems—without the written permission of the publisher.

Picture credits:
Cover: Dreamstime and iStockphoto.com
Maury Aaseng: 32–34, 46–47, 59–61, 74–75
AP Images: 14
Dr. P. Marazzi/Science Photo Library: 11

LIBRARY OF CONGRESS CATALOGING-IN-PUBLICATION DATA

Parks, Peggy J., 1951–
    Impulse control disorders / by Peggy J. Parks.
        p. cm. -- (Compact research)
    Audience: Grade 9 to 12
    Includes bibliographical references and index.
    ISBN 978-1-60152-260-3 (hardback) -- ISBN 1-60152-260-6 (hardback)
    1. Impulse control disorders--Popular works. I. Title.
    RC569.5.I46P37   2013
    362.2'7--dc23
                                                                2012006966

Contents

Foreword

❝Where is the knowledge we have lost in information?❞

—T.S. Eliot, "The Rock."

As modern civilization continues to evolve, its ability to create, store, distribute, and access information expands exponentially. The explosion of information from all media continues to increase at a phenomenal rate. By 2020 some experts predict the worldwide information base will double every 73 days. While access to diverse sources of information and perspectives is paramount to any democratic society, information alone cannot help people gain knowledge and understanding. Information must be organized and presented clearly and succinctly in order to be understood. The challenge in the digital age becomes not the creation of information, but how best to sort, organize, enhance, and present information.

ReferencePoint Press developed the *Compact Research* series with this challenge of the information age in mind. More than any other subject area today, researching current issues can yield vast, diverse, and unqualified information that can be intimidating and overwhelming for even the most advanced and motivated researcher. The *Compact Research* series offers a compact, relevant, intelligent, and conveniently organized collection of information covering a variety of current topics ranging from illegal immigration and deforestation to diseases such as anorexia and meningitis.

The series focuses on three types of information: objective single-author narratives, opinion-based primary source quotations, and facts and statistics. The clearly written objective narratives provide context and reliable background information. Primary source quotes are carefully selected and cited, exposing the reader to differing points of view, and facts and statistics sections aid the reader in evaluating perspectives. Presenting these key types of information creates a richer, more balanced learning experience.

For better understanding and convenience, the series enhances information by organizing it into narrower topics and adding design features that make it easy for a reader to identify desired content. For example, in *Compact Research: Illegal Immigration*, a chapter covering the economic impact of illegal immigration has an objective narrative explaining the various ways the economy is impacted, a balanced section of numerous primary source quotes on the topic, followed by facts and full-color illustrations to encourage evaluation of contrasting perspectives.

The ancient Roman philosopher Lucius Annaeus Seneca wrote, "It is quality rather than quantity that matters." More than just a collection of content, the *Compact Research* series is simply committed to creating, finding, organizing, and presenting the most relevant and appropriate amount of information on a current topic in a user-friendly style that invites, intrigues, and fosters understanding.

Impulse Control Disorders at a Glance

Definition

Impulse control disorders (ICDs) are mental illnesses that involve the inability to resist engaging in behaviors that are harmful to oneself or others.

Primary Types

The five main types of ICDs are trichotillomania (hair pulling), intermittent explosive disorder, pathological gambling, kleptomania (stealing), and pyromania (fire setting).

ICD Episodes

Extreme stress can trigger an ICD episode. Such episodes are often followed by feelings of relief and gratification, although for many people, the pleasurable feelings are soon replaced by guilt, shame, and regret.

Prevalence

The National Institute of Mental Health estimates that 9 percent of Americans suffer from ICDs, although most cases are never reported or diagnosed.

Accompanying Illnesses

ICDs commonly occur with other mental health disorders, such as substance abuse, depression, and anxiety disorders, among others.

Causes

Scientists do not know what causes ICDs but suspect that they develop from a combination of biological and environmental factors.

Quality-of-Life Issues

ICDs can create immense suffering for people affected by them, causing everything from emotional turmoil to family problems, financial ruin, and trouble with law enforcement.

Recovery Challenges

ICD patients are often treated with a combination of therapy and medications. Two problems that inhibit recovery are the large number of sufferers who never seek help and the lack of follow-through with treatment recommendations.

Overview

❝Many people with an impulse control disorder report an urge or a craving state prior to their behavior, as do individuals with substance use disorders prior to drinking or using drugs.❞

—Jon E. Grant and Marc N. Potenza, psychiatrists and coeditors of the *Oxford Handbook of Impulse Control Disorders*.

❝Pathological gambling, compulsive shopping, kleptomania, hypersexuality . . . among other disorders, are characterized by a recurrent urge to perform a repetitive behavior that is gratifying at the moment but causes significant long-term distress and disability.❞

—Elias Aboujaoude and Lorrin M. Koran, psychiatrists at Stanford University School of Medicine and editors of the book *Impulse Control Disorders*.

A 25-year-old Maryland woman named Pam is an editor for a company that publishes educational books for homeschooled children. She enjoys writing and has created a blog called *Trich-y Business*, where she discusses her ongoing struggle with an ICD known as trichotillomania. Aptly named after the Greek word for "hair-pulling madness," trichotillomania involves overwhelming urges to pull out hair from various parts of the body, as Pam writes: "Some pull out scalp hair. Some use fingers, some use tweezers. Some just pull the hair, some rub it between their fingers, some eat it."[1] Pam, who pulls out her eyebrows and eyelashes, says that people with trichotillomania get the urge to pull hair for different reasons, ranging from feeling anxious to just being bored.

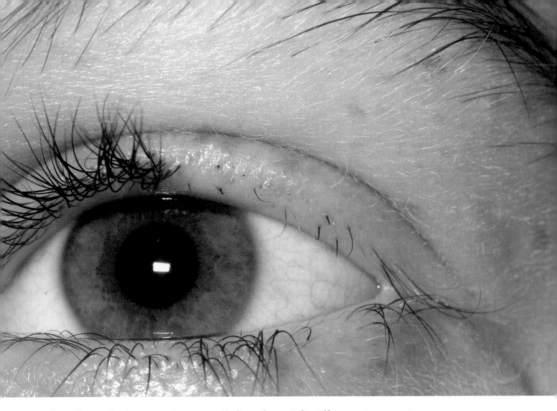

People with the impulse control disorder trichotillomania experience an overwhelming urge to pull out hair from various parts of the body. A young patient's eyelid shows signs of this disorder.

Like others with the disorder, she feels that the hair pulling is out of her control, as she writes: "It's like my hand has a mind of its own."[2]

Pam says that her urges usually start with a slight tingling sensation on the edge of her eyelid where her lashes grow. "If I try to delay the pulling," she says, "I experience symptoms of general anxiety, including slight shaking, shortness of breath, and a feeling in the pit of my stomach, the kind you get when you're really nervous or stressed out." When Pam gives in to the feeling and pulls out one lash, the tension subsides—but only for a moment, and then the urge strikes again to pull more lashes. She writes: "The cycle of anxiety-relief-anxiety continues until my self-loathing overpowers the pulling urge and I angrily grab a jar of Vaseline and try to soothe my screaming eyelids."[3]

What Are Impulse Control Disorders?

The words *pathological* and *compulsive* are consistently used whenever ICDs are discussed, and both aptly describe the disorders. A pathological condition is one that stems from physical or mental disease, whereas a compulsion is the state of being compelled, or acting on strong impulses or urges. Thus, ICDs are mental illnesses in which sufferers lack the ability to resist an intense impulse, drive, or temptation to do something harmful to themselves or others.

> ICDs are mental illnesses in which sufferers lack the ability to resist an intense impulse, drive, or temptation to do something harmful to themselves or others.

Impulsivity itself is not uncommon, nor is it necessarily bad. Most people are impulsive from time to time, rather than giving careful thought and consideration to everything they do. When a person is said to have acted impulsively, it means that he or she did something on a whim, like making a spur-of-the-moment decision to get a tattoo, shave his or her head, or hop on a plane and fly to the Caribbean for the weekend. Although such impulsive actions may cause some regret later, they are generally not harmful. That is how they differ from ICDs, which involve a complete absence of control over impulses. In an article on the website Psych Central, physician Daniel Ploskin writes: "As humans, the ability to control our impulses—or urges—helps distinguish us from other species and marks our psychological maturity. Most of us take our ability to think before we act for granted. But this isn't easy for people who have problems controlling their impulses."[4]

Primary ICDs

The American Psychiatric Association (APA) officially recognizes five ICDs in its *Diagnostic and Statistical Manual of Mental Disorders* (DSM), the most recent of which was released in July 2000. Often called the bible of psychiatric disorders, the DSM provides physicians with the criteria they need to diagnose every type of mental illness. The ICDs included in the DSM include trichotillomania, intermittent explosive disorder (aggressive outbursts of anger), pathological gambling, kleptomania (uncontrollable stealing), and pyromania (habitual fire setting). The criteria for each differ based on the nature of the condition, but people who suffer from them share one thing in common: the inability to resist over-whelming urges.

One of the most common ICDs is pathological gambling, which is characterized by persistent, destructive patterns of gambling behavior. This does not pertain to someone who enjoys occasional outings to casinos or purchases a lottery ticket from time to time. In contrast, pathological gamblers are preoccupied with gambling to the point of being plagued by a desperate, driving need to gamble. Even immediately after a gambling expedition, many pathological gamblers are already obsessing over their next venture and are thinking about ways to get more money—even if it involves lying to friends and family or committing crimes such as forgery, theft, or embezzlement. Laura M. Letson, who is with the New York Council on Problem Gambling, writes: "The majority of people who participate in gambling view it as a social activity that does not negatively impact their lives, and, win or lose, they walk away unaffected. When an addicted gambler's life begins to spiral out of control, however, he or she will often engage in desperate acts in attempts to get even or to continue the 'action.'"[5]

> People with intermittent explosive disorder also feel like their lives are out of control, but in their case, uncontrollable impulses lead to blinding fits of rage.

People with intermittent explosive disorder also feel like their lives are out of control, but in their case, uncontrollable impulses lead to blinding fits of rage. These aggressive behaviors, which often involve violence, tend to be grossly out of proportion to the seriousness of a particular situation. A person who experiences road rage after being passed by a car on the highway, for example, might suffer from this disorder. According to the Mayo Clinic, people with intermittent explosive disorder may attack others with the intent of causing bodily injury and destroying possessions. The group writes: "Explosive eruptions, usually lasting 10 to 20 minutes, often result in injuries and the deliberate destruction of property."[6]

Gamblers try their luck at the slot machines in a New York casino. Pathological gambling is a common impulse control disorder. It is characterized by persistent, destructive patterns of gambling behavior.

Other Members of the ICD Family

Along with the five officially designated ICDs, the APA also recognizes a sixth category known as impulse control disorder not otherwise specified. This is reserved for physicians to use when they determine that a patient's condition is related to problems with impulse control but does not meet the full criteria for ICDs as described in the DSM. Because the APA does not dictate which conditions are included in this category, a diagnosis is often made based on the opinions of mental health professionals. Disorders that are commonly included in this category are compulsive sexual behavior (or hypersexuality), compulsive skin picking (or dermatillomania), and compulsive buying (or shopping).

Many physicians also consider self-mutilation to be an ICD, because those who suffer from it intentionally injure themselves in an attempt to relieve stress. The New York University Langone Medical Center calls self-mutilation a "severe impulse control disorder," saying that it involves "any form of self-harm inflicted on your body without the intent to commit suicide."[7] People who self-mutilate do so in various ways, the most common of which is cutting the skin with razor blades, shards of glass, or other sharp objects. Other forms of self-mutilation include burning; sticking the skin with needles, pins, or nails; biting fingers, lips, arms, or hands; and repeatedly banging the head on a hard surface.

Compulsive sexual behavior involves out-of-control sexual feelings and behaviors. People with this condition often describe mood states such as anxiety, depression, and boredom that can only be alleviated through sexual fantasies or sexual behaviors that are inappropriate and often considered immoral. According to Reef Karim, a psychiatrist who directs the Control Center, a self-control and addiction treatment facility in Beverly Hills, California, typical compulsive sexual behavior sufferers have "repeatedly tried to control their sexual behavior (masturbation, pornography, sexual behavior with consenting adults, strip clubs, prostitution, cybersex, etc.) but they simply can't do it."[8]

Emotional Highs and Lows

Although each ICD has its own unique characteristics, a typical warning sign is the sudden onset of stress or arousal. Often this happens with little or no warning, as California psychologist Nicole Stelter writes: "These unpleasant feelings can feel 'out of the blue' and not precipitated by anything in a person's environment."[9] Stelter goes on to say that the tension continues to build and grow stronger until the person feels powerless against urges that bring relief.

For someone with kleptomania, the buildup of tension will inevitably lead to stealing, while it will send a pathological gambler rushing to the nearest casino. Someone with pyromania feels an overwhelming need to set fires and then personally witness the aftermath—even if the act has resulted in tragedy. French psychiatrists Candice Germain and Michel Lejoyeux explain: "Pyromaniacs are usually indifferent to the material or human consequences of a fire they have caused. Some may experience a certain pleasure while viewing the resulting destruction."[10]

Once an impulsive act has been completed, the typical reaction is pleasure, relief, and gratification. For many sufferers, however, these positive feelings are short-lived. Because people with ICDs realize that their behavior is abnormal and unacceptable, they often feel crushing guilt, shame, and sorrow over their actions. According to Jon E. Grant, a psychiatrist who codirects the Impulse Control Disorders Clinic at the University of Minnesota, these feelings of remorse are especially prevalent among those with pyromania or kleptomania because these acts "cut against people's beliefs about moral ways of living. People are devastated to realize that they're breaking the law and going against the kind of person they think they should be."[11]

ICD Sufferers

According to the National Institute of Mental Health, an estimated 9 percent of men and women in the United States have one or more ICD. In females compulsive buying is most common, while compulsive sexual behavior and pathological gambling primarily affect men. The exact prevalence of ICDs, however, is unknown. A major hindrance to the compilation of accurate statistics is that most people with these disorders are never diagnosed, often because their fear, guilt, and shame deter them from seeking help. Another limitation of determining the actual incidence of ICDs is that research on some of these disorders has been scarce, although in recent years that has started to change. In their book *Impulse Control Disorders*, Elias Aboujaoude and Lorrin M. Koran write: "The last decade has brought the impulse control disorders (ICDs) much-needed attention and has seen the accumulation of a modest body of clinical research results."[12]

> For someone with kleptomania, the buildup of tension will inevitably lead to stealing, while it will send a pathological gambler rushing to the nearest casino.

To evaluate the prevalence of ICDs among college students, Grant conducted a research project with his colleague, Brian L. Odlaug. The study, which was published in the 2010 issue of the *Journal of Clinical Psychiatry*, involved nearly 800 young adults from two private midwestern colleges. Based on information from comprehensive questionnaires, 10.4 percent of participants met the criteria for at least one ICD. The two most commonly reported ICDs were trichotillomania (4 percent of participants) and compulsive sexual behavior (3.7 percent). At less than half a percent prevalence, kleptomania was the least common.

Multiple Mental Health Issues

Studies with ICD patients have shown that many suffer from other accompanying mental health disorders, which is known as comorbidity. Substance abuse is among the most common conditions associated with ICDs, according to a study published in the September 2010 issue of the *American Journal of Drug and Alcohol Abuse*. At the conclusion of the study, the researchers determined that substance abuse affects from 35 to 64 percent of pathological gamblers, 64 percent of those with compulsive sexual behavior, and up to 50 percent of kleptomaniacs. What remains unclear, though, is whether people with an ICD turn to substance abuse as a way of dealing with unbearable stress or if an existing substance abuse problem leads to impulsive behaviors. As researchers continue to explore the connection between ICDs and substance abuse, they hope the answer to this and other questions will be revealed.

> **Scientists have been aware of impulse-related conditions for centuries, but the cause of ICDs remains unknown.**

ICDs are also common among those with psychiatric conditions such as borderline personality disorder, depression, anxiety disorders, and bipolar disorder. The latter was the focus of a study published in July 2011 by Turkish researchers, whose goal was to evaluate ICD comorbidity among 124 patients with a severe form of bipolar disorder. At the conclusion of the study, the team determined that over 27 percent of the bipolar patients also suffered from one or more ICDs. The most prevalent was pathological skin picking, followed by compulsive buying, intermittent explosive disorder, and trichotillomania (in that order).

What Causes Impulse Control Disorders?

Scientists have been aware of impulse-related conditions for centuries, but the cause of ICDs remains unknown. As with most mental illnesses, ICDs probably develop from multiple causes, as Ploskin writes: "Many

> Many mental health professionals say that ICDs are seriously underdiagnosed, in large part because so many sufferers never seek treatment. Another factor is that not all health care professionals acknowledge ICDs as true mental health disorders.

things probably play a role, including physical or biological, psychological or emotional and cultural or societal factors."[13]

One theory that has long been a topic of scientific interest is the possible relationship between ICDs and brain chemistry. Scientists are particularly curious about the role of neurotransmitters, which are chemical messengers that enable brain cells (known as neurons) to communicate with each other. Researchers Justin A. Brewer and Marc N. Potenza write: "Consistently, data from human and animal studies suggest that multiple brain regions and neurotransmitter systems contribute to impulsive behaviors."[14] One neurotransmitter that has been the focus of much research is serotonin, which is involved with mood, sleep, appetite, memory, learning, and inhibition of behavior. Many scientists are convinced that low serotonin levels can significantly affect a person's ability to control impulses.

What Are the Effects of Impulse Control Disorders?

Poor quality of life is an unfortunate reality for many people who suffer from ICDs. Although they agonize over the inability to control their impulses and urges, they often feel like a slave to them. People with kleptomania, for instance, cannot make themselves stop stealing. Yet at the same time, they live in fear that they will be caught and sent to jail, which will lead to public embarrassment and bring shame to their families. Those with compulsive buying disorder often rack up thousands of dollars in debt, which can lead to severe financial problems. Indiana University professor Ruth Engs explains: "They are often in denial about the problem. Because they cannot pay their bills their credit rating suffers, they have collection agencies attempting to get what is owed, may have legal, social and relationship problems."[15]

One of the most devastating ICDs is pathological gambling. People who are unable to control their urges to gamble may turn to crime after exhausting their own money, lose their jobs and homes, and destroy their relationships with family and friends. Roxanne Dryden-Edwards, a psychiatrist from Montgomery County, Maryland, writes: "Harmful effects that compulsive gambling can have on the individual include financial problems ranging from high debt, bankruptcy or poverty, to legal problems resulting from theft to prostitution, to wanting, attempting or completing suicide."[16]

Arriving at a Diagnosis

Many mental health professionals say that ICDs are seriously underdiagnosed, in large part because so many sufferers never seek treatment. Another factor is that not all health care professionals acknowledge ICDs as true mental health disorders. Referring to compulsive sexual behavior, Karim explains: "Some physicians see the intense suffering and loss of relationships, marriages, jobs and even one's freedom because of the disorder. Other physicians, however, feel that the disorder is just made up to describe bad behavior."[17] When someone seeks medical help, a physician performs a complete physical examination and often conducts a variety of tests to rule out other conditions that could be causing poor impulse control. If no other illnesses or disorders are found, he or she will likely refer the patient to a mental health specialist for further evaluation.

> **From bouts of explosive anger to the compulsive need to pull out one's hair, steal, gamble, or set fires, ICDs are serious mental illnesses.**

Based on symptoms described by the patient, and a thorough mental health screening, a psychiatrist or psychologist will usually be able to tell whether the person suffers from an ICD. In order to make a formal diagnosis, though, diagnostic criteria from the DSM must be used. For kleptomania, these criteria are composed of five symptoms: persistent failure to resist impulses to steal objects that are not needed for personal use or for their monetary value; an increasing sense of tension immediately before committing the theft; pleasure, gratification, or relief at the time the theft is committed; the stealing is not committed to express anger or revenge, nor is it in response to delusions or hallucinations; and the stealing cannot be attributed to other mental illnesses such as conduct disorder or antisocial personality disorder.

Can People Overcome Impulse Control Disorders?

Mental health professionals say that many ICD patients have a good chance of recovering from their disorder if they seek help. This depends, however, on the specific ICD, the patient's motivation to conquer it, and his or her willingness to diligently follow a recommended treatment plan—with the latter being a major hurdle. No matter how badly ICD sufferers may want to change, the idea of giving up behaviors that have become coping mechanisms is often more than they can handle. Speaking of pathological gamblers, Dryden-Edwards writes: "One of the challenges of treatment of compulsive gambling is that as many as two-thirds of people who begin treatment for this disorder discontinue treatment prematurely."[18]

Depending on the individual disorder, treatment for ICDs usually involves a combination of psychotherapy and medications. Since no drugs have been approved by the US Food and Drug Administration to specifically treat ICDs, physicians often prescribe antidepressants or mood-stabilizing medications as part of a patient's treatment program. A February 2011 paper by Grant, Odlaug, and colleague Liana Schreiber discussed the various ICDs and drugs used to treat them, such as an antidepressant known as fluvoxamine that has helped many who suffer from compulsive skin picking.

Out of Control

From bouts of explosive anger to the compulsive need to pull out one's hair, steal, gamble, or set fires, ICDs are serious mental illnesses. They begin with urges that continue to build until they seem unbearable and often result in behaviors that are harmful and destructive. With the right treatment, patients can make substantial progress, and some are able to overcome their ICDs. As scientists continue to explore these puzzling disorders, research may yield discoveries that benefit ICD sufferers and give them hope for a better future.

What Are Impulse Control Disorders?

> ❝Impulse control disorders occur when impulsive behaviors get the best of you.❞

—Michael Roizen, a physician from Cleveland, Ohio, and the author of eight books, including *You: The Owner's Manual for Teens.*

> ❝Still considered, unfortunately, by many researchers to be only of limited interest, research has generated a remarkable amount of data supporting the claim that the impulse control disorders are truly common and disabling behaviors.❞

—Jon E. Grant, a psychiatrist who codirects the Impulse Control Disorders Clinic at the University of Minnesota and who is an expert on ICDs.

For hundreds of years physicians have observed and written about disorders that are characterized by a lack of impulse control. During the 1700s German physician Franz Joseph Gall reported that several prominent men, including an Italian king, habitually stole items for no apparent reason. In the nineteenth century French psychiatrist Jean-Étienne Esquirol coined the term *monomania* to describe patients who committed impulsive acts even though their minds seemed to be otherwise intact. Says Jon E. Grant: "[Esquirol] would see people who could control their behavior in all other spheres of life—they could work, they could run a household, but they had this one area that was out of control."[19]

Another French psychiatrist, Raoul Leroy, wrote a paper in 1904 titled "Pyromania, a Psychosis of Puberty," in which he described a peculiar mental illness that involved intentional fire setting. Based on his observations, Leroy determined that the disorder known as pyromania tended to affect adolescents, most often girls. A March 1905 article in the British medical journal *Lancet* summarized his views about youth who were affected by the disorder:

> These feeble-minded delinquents are prone to set fire to buildings or other objects in revenge against their owners or in some cases merely to amuse themselves with the spectacle. A few cases, says Dr. Leroy, suffer from the influence of an obsession which irresistibly impels them to such acts, such cases forming a special form of insanity to which the term "pyromania" is applied. True cases of pyromania manifest themselves for the first time at the period of puberty.[20]

A Burning Need

Although the disparaging term *feeble-minded* disappeared from psychiatric language long ago, Leroy's description of pyromania was largely accurate. Derived from the Greek words *pyr*, meaning "fire," and *mania*, meaning "madness," pyromania involves irresistible urges and typically develops during adolescence. In a February 2011 article in *Frontiers in Psychiatry*, researchers state that the disorder's prevalence has not been well established, but their paper cites studies of hospitalized adolescents, of whom 3 to 6 percent fit the APA's criteria for pyromania. Additionally, pyromania is no longer believed to be most prevalent among females; in fact, research suggests the opposite. The researchers write: "Usually, pyromania develops during adolescence and is more common in males."[21]

Although people who commit arson (the deliberate, criminal act of setting fires) are sometimes thought to have pyromania, this is not usually the case. The behavior of pyromaniacs stems from overwhelming urges rather than motives such as monetary gain (fraudulent collection of money from insurance policies), acts of revenge, violent protests, or terrorist activities. Psychiatrists Candice Germain and Michel Lejoyeux refer to pyromania as an impulsive behavior that leads to fire setting "without an identifiable motive other than taking pleasure in viewing the fire and its effects."[22] They add that pyromania shares many characteristics with other ICDs, including a strong urge or craving prior to engaging in the behavior, finding the behavior pleasurable, repeating the behavior despite negative consequences, diminished control over what they do, and increased frequency and intensity of the behavior.

> " During the 1700s German physician Franz Joseph Gall reported that several prominent men, including an Italian king, habitually stole items for no apparent reason. "

Because pyromaniacs intentionally set fires and are often responsible for property damage, injuries, and even deaths, the idea that they are mentally ill is highly controversial. Germain and Lejoyeux explain: "The validity of pyromania as a psychiatric diagnosis continues to be questioned in that some do not believe that this mental disorder really exists."[23] It is not uncommon for people to assume that pyromaniacs are fully responsible for their destructive actions and should be held accountable for those actions when they break the law. This continues to be debated among the general public, in the courts, and even among mental health professionals.

Driven to Steal

Kleptomania is another controversial ICD because people with the disorder are often assumed to be common thieves or professional shoplifters. The difference, though, is that episodes of kleptomania usually occur spontaneously, without advance planning or obvious motive. Also, kleptomaniacs do not steal because they need or want the objects they take, as the Mayo Clinic explains: "Unlike typical shoplifters, people with kleptomania don't compulsively steal for personal gain. Nor do they steal as a way to exact revenge. They steal simply because the urge is so powerful that they can't resist it. This urge makes them feel uncomfortably anxious, tense or aroused. To soothe these feelings, they steal."[24] Kleptomaniacs steal from a variety of people and places, most notably

> **Because pyromaniacs intentionally set fires and are often responsible for property damage, injuries, and even deaths, the idea that they are mentally ill is highly controversial.**

public establishments such as stores and supermarkets, but also from family, friends, and acquaintances. "During the theft," says the Mayo Clinic, "they feel relief and gratification. Afterward, though, they may feel enormous guilt, remorse, self-loathing and fear of arrest. But the urge comes back, and the kleptomania cycle repeats itself."[25]

A woman named Shelley can personally relate to these extreme mood swings, from feeling elation and relief to guilt and deep shame. She began shoplifting when she was 16 years old and describes how she felt after stealing the first time: "My whole nervous system was excited. It was like coming close to the fire and then escaping the danger; the relief and gratification were overwhelming." These positive feelings did not last, however. As is typical of people with kleptomania (and other ICDs), the sense of pleasure soon gave way to feelings of disgust and self-loathing, and Shelley was overcome by the "shame of knowing that what I was doing was immoral and harmful to society."[26]

Gambling as an Obsession

Since 1980 pathological gambling has been included in the DSM as one of the primary ICDs, although the criteria have been revised several times over the years. Today, in order for someone to be diagnosed as a pathological gambler, he or she must exhibit at least five of the following symptoms: being preoccupied with gambling; needing to gamble with higher and higher amounts of money; repeatedly being unsuccessful at trying to control gambling; becoming restless or irritable when attempting to control gambling; gambling used as a way to escape problems or relieve feelings of helplessness, guilt, anxiety, or depression; "chasing losses," or attempting to recoup lost money by gambling more; lying about the seriousness of the problem; committing illegal acts such as forgery, fraud, theft, or embezzlement to finance gambling; jeopardizing or losing relationships, jobs, or educational/career opportunities; and relying on others for money when the gambling-related financial situation becomes desperate.

Research has shown that pathological gamblers are most often middle-aged men, but males and females of all ages and all walks of life suffer from the disorder. A woman named Kristy lives with the frustration of knowing that her elderly mother is a pathological gambler. "You can't imagine what it's like," says Kristy, "to follow her around for hours while she stops at ATM after ATM to clean out her checking account, or to find out that she lied to a sibling in order to guilt them into giving her money for some bogus bill."[27]

Inexplicable Rage

Even though pathological gambling and intermittent explosive disorder are very different conditions, the common thread between them (as with all ICDs) is uncontrollable impulses. In recent years the latter has received a great deal of news coverage, in large part because of highly publicized tirades by celebrities such as Mel Gibson and Charlie Sheen. Although it is not clear whether those actors suffer from intermittent explosive disorder, their behavior has raised awareness of the condition—and heightened controversy over whether it is really a mental illness. Society tends to be intolerant of someone who cannot control his or her anger and has a reputation for being abusive and violent. As the authors of an April 2011 article in *Harvard Mental Health Letter* write: "The condition remains controversial, especially when it is diagnosed in an individual being held to account for violent actions."[28]

> " According to mental health professionals who treat people with intermittent explosive disorder, these patients are unable to control the urges that are at the root of their aggressive outbursts. "

Yet according to mental health professionals who treat people with intermittent explosive disorder, these patients are unable to control the urges that are at the root of their aggressive outbursts. As with kleptomania, trichotillomania, and other

ICDs, impulses become overwhelming and seemingly impossible to ignore. Psychologist Stephen A. Diamond says that sufferers describe these repeated bouts of rage in different ways, including seizures, spells, or attacks that "build up to an intolerable crescendo of tension and arousal, reach a point of no return, and are, at first, followed by pleasurable relaxation and relief. But after the fact, the violent perpetrator may . . . feel remorseful or ashamed of their bad behavior or evil deed."[29]

> **ICDs are some of the most difficult, frustrating mental illnesses—not only for sufferers, but also for those who care about them.**

In July 2011 a man posted an online comment about his personal battle with intermittent explosive disorder, saying, "I wish I could handle stress and frustration like other people. I can't."[30] Even though the man is well educated and has extensive work experience, he has not been able to keep a job for very long. He admits that on numerous occasions he was "scary and difficult to be near," exploding in rage at even the most trivial situations. He writes: "My wife didn't like the way I put up a clothes-line post. I started screaming and throwing things. My son didn't seem to be responsible when interviewing and selecting colleges. I had to visit a psychiatrist, since I had murderous thoughts." Even though the man once had a lucrative job, he now lives on Social Security disability payments, making a fraction of what he used to earn. "It's what I do to live life on life's terms," he says, "I'm lucky that I can drive around and am not in an institution."[31]

Common Misdiagnoses

All ICDs are well defined in the DSM, with criteria varying based on the individual disorder. Yet because these disorders are often misunderstood, it is not uncommon for them to be diagnosed incorrectly. Grant writes: "When combined with lack of knowledge regarding the clinical characteristics of impulse control disorders, the likelihood of misdiagnosis is considerable."[32] Two conditions that are often mistaken for ICDs are obsessive-compulsive disorder and attention-deficit/hyperactivity disorder, since poor impulse control is symptomatic of both.

Epilepsy is another illness that may involve impulse control symptoms, such as uncharacteristic outbursts of rage. A 17-year-old boy from Canada sought help for severe anger issues, and the doctors initially thought he suffered from intermittent explosive disorder. The boy had become progressively angrier over the past six months, and his bouts of rage seemed to erupt suddenly, without any obvious provocation. In a 2011 case report, physicians Wendy K. Ng and Jose Mejia explain: "This was accompanied by escalating impulsive, recurrent and constant thoughts about violently killing anyone that he saw, predominantly using weapons such as knives, swords or guns. . . . His thoughts were focused on his preoccupation with killing people."[33] On at least two occasions, the boy was filled with such blinding rage while alone at home that he started ripping furniture apart and breaking it into pieces.

Ng and Mejia suspected the boy suffered from intermittent explosive disorder. But before they made a diagnosis, they put him through a number of tests to rule out other disorders that might have caused his symptoms. One of the tests was an electroencephalogram, which measured and recorded the electrical activity of the boy's brain. Based on test results, the physicians determined that the boy suffered from epilepsy, which was the cause of his explosive behavior. Ng and Mejia write: "This case reminds us of the possibility that a seizure disorder may mimic the symptoms of IED [intermittent explosive disorder]."[34]

No Easy Answers

ICDs are some of the most difficult, frustrating mental illnesses—not only for sufferers, but also for those who care about them. Some of these disorders are controversial, with many people convinced that they are indicative of bad behavior and lack of self-control, rather than being pathological conditions. Mental health professionals who treat patients with ICDs argue that their actions stem from urges that come upon them suddenly and are too overpowering to ignore. As more is learned about these disorders, they will undoubtedly become better understood—but whether the controversies surrounding them will ever be resolved is unknown.

What Are Impulse Control Disorders?

Primary Source Quotes

66 **One of the hallmarks of ICDs is that they often occur in people who have shown no inclination to impulsive or socially inappropriate behavior in the past, and reflect an unmistakable change from a patient's normal personality.** 99

—Andrew Siderowf, "What Are Impulse Control Disorders in PD Patients and Why Is This Important?," *On the Blog*, National Parkinson Foundation, April 28, 2011. www.parkinson.org.

Siderowf is the medical director of the National Parkinson Foundation Center of Excellence at the University of Pennsylvania Parkinson's Disease and Movement Disorders Center.

66 **Controversy surrounds both substance-related and impulse-control disorders because our society sometimes believes that both these problems are simply a lack of 'will.'** 99

—V. Mark Durand and David H. Barlow, *Essentials of Abnormal Psychology*. Belmont, CA: Wadsworth, 2009.

Durand is a psychologist from St. Petersburg, Florida, and Barlow is a psychologist from Boston.

* Editor's Note: While the definition of a primary source can be narrowly or broadly defined, for the purposes of Compact Research, a primary source consists of: 1) results of original research presented by an organization or researcher; 2) eyewitness accounts of events, personal experience, or work experience; 3) first-person editorials offering pundits' opinions; 4) government officials presenting political plans and/or policies; 5) representatives of organizations presenting testimony or policy.

66 Unlike arsonists, pyromaniacs start fires to induce euphoria, and often fixate on institutions of fire control like fire stations and firefighters.**99**

—Better Tomorrow Treatment Center, "Pyromania," *New Beginnings for a Better Tomorrow* (blog), June 8, 2010. http://abtomorrow.blogspot.com.

The Better Tomorrow Treatment Center is an addiction recovery facility located in Southern California.

66 Road rage, domestic abuse, and angry outbursts or temper tantrums that involve throwing or breaking objects may be signs of intermittent explosive disorder (IED).**99**

—Mayo Clinic, "Intermittent Explosive Disorder," June 10, 2010. www.mayoclinic.com.

The Mayo Clinic is a world-renowned medical care facility headquartered in Rochester, Minnesota.

66 Officially, trichotillomania is considered an impulse control disorder similar to kleptomania, pathological gambling or pyromania. It involves a recurrent and overwhelming urge to pull out one's hair, often leading to patches of baldness.**99**

—Paul Latimer, "Trichotillomania," Castanet, July 27, 2011. www.castanet.net.

Latimer is a psychiatrist, medical researcher, and writer from British Columbia, Canada.

66 Given that DSM is essentially the reference book to define a mental disorder, the diagnosis of hypersexuality disorder means, to put it crudely, that if the patient has more sex than the doctor thinks is appropriate, then the patient could be labelled mentally ill.**99**

—Shirah Vollmer, "Hypersexuality: DSM 5, Are You Kidding?," *Musings of Dr. Vollmer* (blog), February 15, 2010. http://shirahvollmermd.wordpress.com.

Vollmer is a psychiatrist from Los Angeles, California.

66 Unlike shoplifting, people who suffer from kleptomania do not steal for personal gain; they steal because of the urge. The urge makes these individuals feel anxious, tense, or aroused, and they steal to put these feelings at bay. 99

—Dhiren Patel, "How to Deal with a Kleptomaniac," Solace Counseling, April 28, 2011. www.solacecounseling.com.

Patel is a psychologist from Dallas, Texas.

66 Individuals who suffer from what is termed an 'impulse-control disorder' often steal items for which they have no use. Consequently, they give away or throw away the proceeds of their crimes. 99

—Stanton E. Samenow, "Kleptomania: A Reality or Psychiatric Invention?," *Inside the Criminal Mind* (blog), *Psychology Today*, March 4, 2011. www.psychologytoday.com.

Samenow is a clinical psychologist from Alexandria, Virginia.

Facts and Illustrations

What Are Impulse Control Disorders?

- A 2010 paper in the *Journal of Clinical Psychiatry* states that ICDs affect an estimated **8.9 percent** of the US population.

- According to forensic psychiatrist Michael Menaster, fewer than **5 percent** of shoplifters meet the criteria for kleptomania.

- In a May 2011 online poll by the Shulman Center for Compulsive Theft, Spending & Hoarding, **25 percent** of respondents said they had stolen over **1,000 times**.

- Psychiatrist Daniel A. Plotkin states that only about **1 percent** of people who have been arrested for arson are diagnosed with pyromania.

- A study published in March 2011 by researchers from the Research Institute on Addictions found that after age 21, **problem gambling** is significantly more common among adults in the United States than alcohol addiction.

- The Mayo Clinic states that trichotillomania usually develops during adolescence, most often between the ages of **11 and 13**.

- According to the mental health and addiction website ChooseHelp, teenagers are more likely than adults to develop a gambling problem, and an estimated **10 percent** of teens from grades 7 to 12 are already problem gamblers.

ICDs and Their Characteristics

The American Psychiatric Association (APA) officially recognizes five impulse control disorders: pathological gambling, kleptomania, trichotillomania, intermittent explosive disorder, and pyromania, which are shown here along with their common characteristics.

Impulse Control Disorder	Characteristics
Pathological gambling	Persistent, repetitive patterns of destructive gambling behaviors.
Kleptomania	Repetitive, uncontrollable stealing of items not needed for personal use.
Trichotillomania	Repetitive hair-pulling that causes noticeable hair loss.
Intermittent explosive disorder	Recurrent, often violent outbursts of aggressiveness, which result in assaultive acts upon people or property.
Pyromania	Deliberate, purposeful fire setting on more than one occasion.

Source: Liana Schreiber, Brian L. Odlaug, and Jon E. Grant, "Impulse Control Disorders: Updated Review of Clinical Characteristics and Pharmacological Management," *Frontiers in Psychiatry*, February 21, 2011. www.frontiersin.org.

- In a 2011 paper, psychiatrists Wendy K. Ng and Jose Mejia estimate that **1 to 2 percent** of the population suffers from intermittent explosive disorder.

- According to the National Council on Problem Gambling, an estimated **2 million** people in the United States meet the criteria for pathological gambling.

ICD Types Differ Among Males, Females

Both males and females suffer from impulse control disorders, but the types often differ based on gender. This graph shows the ICDs that were found to be most common among 791 college students during a study that was published in 2010.

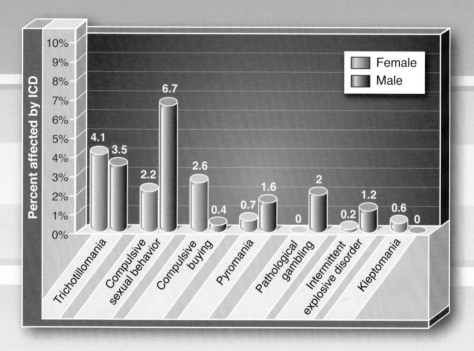

Note: Scale only goes up to 10 percent.

Source: Brian L. Odlaug and Jon E. Grant, "Impulse-Control Disorders in a College Sample: Results from the Self-Administered Minnesota Impulse Disorders Interview (MIDI)," *Journal of Clinical Psychiatry*, 2010. www.ncbi.nlm.nih.gov.

- According to Eastern Virginia Medical School psychiatrists David R. Spiegel and Lindsey Finklea, pathological skin picking most often affects females in their **teens to late thirties**.

- The Trichotillomania Learning Center estimates that trichotillomania affects from **2 to 4 percent** of the population, or up to 10 million Americans.

Most Problem Gamblers Are Middle-Aged Adults

People of all ages and all walks of life can develop serious gambling problems. According to a study published in April 2011 by researchers from the University of Buffalo's Research Institute on Addictions, those most likely to be problem gamblers* are between the ages of 31 and 40.

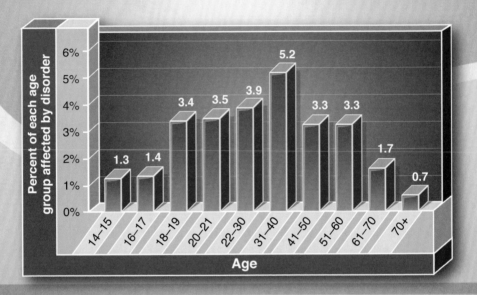

Note: Scale only goes up to 6 percent.

*Met three or more of the American Psychiatric Association's criteria for problem gambling in the past year.

Source: John W. Welte et al., "Gambling and Problem Gambling Across the Lifespan," *Journal of Gambling Studies,* April 18, 2011.

- According to forensic psychiatrist Michael Menaster, the estimated prevalence of pathological gambling is **3 percent**.

- The Trichotillomania Learning Center states that **80 to 90 percent** of trichotillomania cases among adults are women.

What Causes Impulse Control Disorders?

> 66The causes of impulsiveness and the development of effective treatment approaches continue to challenge researchers who specialize in exploring human behavior.99

—Bill Baker, a marriage and family therapist from Birmingham, Alabama.

> 66The body of evidence collected by our laboratory and others suggest a strong influence of genetic components on impulsive behavior.99

—David A. Nielsen and Dmitri Proudnikov, psychiatrists, and Mary Jeanne Kreek, a physician who specializes in addictive diseases.

Scientists have proposed numerous theories about ICDs but are still puzzled about the cause. No one knows with any certainty why some people pull out their hair, steal items they neither want nor need, gamble compulsively, start fires, or are unable to keep themselves from exploding in rage. Research continues to yield promising clues about how ICDs develop, and more will likely be revealed in the coming years. ICD specialists generally agree that multiple causes are involved, as Jon E. Grant explains: "Scientists recognize that the cause of impulse control disorders is most likely multi-factorial—that is, genetic, developmental, biological, and environmental factors all play crucial roles. On the individual level, however, how much weight to assign to any or all of these variables is still unknown."[35]

Clues Within the Brain

Scientists who study ICDs believe that alterations in brain chemistry could play a significant role in the development of these disorders. The most powerful organ in the human body, the brain controls everything from the ability to blink one's eyes to walking, talking, learning, remembering, and feeling emotions. These functions are possible because of the brain's highly complex network of neurons, whose neurotransmitters enable ongoing communication via rapid-fire electrical signals. A June 2011 *Science Daily* article refers to this intricate process as "a dance of chemical messages so delicate that missteps often lead to neurological dysfunction."[36] If the "dance" is interrupted, meaning that something has interfered with the normal balance of neurotransmitters, the brain cannot function properly. This can have any number of adverse effects, including the loss of ability to control impulsive behaviors.

One of the most vital neurotransmitters is serotonin, because of its involvement in so many different brain functions. Serotonin helps regulate mood, appetite, sleep, perception of pain, emotional regulation, and inhibition. Deficiencies of the chemical have been implicated in numerous mental illnesses, including ICDs. This was the focus of a paper that appears in the book *Oxford Handbook of Impulse Control Disorders*. The paper's authors discuss a variety of biological factors that are associated with ICDs, with one of the most profound being brain chemistry. Their research has involved analyzing multiple studies, some of which examined the close relationship between serotonin and impulse control. They explain: "Pioneering studies demonstrated that low levels of serotonin . . . are associated with impulsive behaviors."[37]

> " Scientists who study ICDs believe that alterations in brain chemistry could play a significant role in the development of these disorders. "

The researchers discovered that serotonin deficiencies affect the function of the frontal cortex, which is also called the frontal lobe. As the name implies, this is the front part of the brain. It is responsible for higher-level thinking, planning, judgment, problem solving, and impulse control. The frontal cortex has been a focus of research for years because of its crucial role in brain function—and the disastrous effects that can result from damage to it. According to Harvard Medical School, this part of the brain has been closely associated with impulsive aggression such as the type displayed by people with intermittent explosive disorder.

An especially famous historical account of the effects of frontal cortex damage is the story of Phineas Gage, a railroad foreman who was gravely injured on September 13, 1848. Along with his crew, Gage was excavating rocks in preparation for laying railroad track when a massive explosion sent an iron rod hurtling through the air like a missile. The rod was driven into the side of Gage's face and exited through the top of his head. Miraculously, he survived, but the injury had dramatic effects on his personality. He changed from being a friendly, well-liked man to one who was obnoxious and inconsiderate, known for profanity-laced tirades that were formerly out of character for him. An account of the incident was published in an 1868 issue of the *Bulletin of the Massachusetts Medical Society*, which stated: "His mind was radically changed, so decidedly that his friends and acquaintances said he was 'no longer Gage.'"[38]

Over 150 years later, using precise measurements obtained from Gage's skull, scientists re-created his brain with computer technology and found severe damage to much of his frontal cortex. The discovery confirmed the team's suspicion that damage to this part of the brain can cause striking changes in personality (including lack of impulse control), while leaving other neurological functions intact.

The Feel-Good Chemical

As scientists have continued to study the brain for clues about what causes ICDs, the neurotransmitter dopamine has piqued their interest. Sometimes called the "feel-good chemical," dopamine regulates emotional response, motivation, and ability to experience pleasure and pain. Research has shown that when levels of dopamine are higher than normal, this can result in a number of physical and mental problems, including lack of inhibition and poor impulse control.

According to Samantha Smithstein, a psychologist and cofounder of the Pathways Institute for Impulse Control in San Francisco, dopamine creates a reward circuit in the brain in response to highly pleasurable or intense experiences. In this way dopamine "records" that certain experiences are important enough for lasting memories to be created. Also, as Smithstein writes, "the more powerful the experience is, the stronger the message is to the brain to repeat the activity."[39] In keeping with that theory, someone could have the urge to keep repeating a particular act (such as gambling or stealing) in order to feel the pleasurable rush that dopamine provides.

> **Research has shown that when levels of dopamine are higher than normal, this can result in a number of physical and mental problems, including lack of inhibition and poor impulse control.**

The connection between dopamine and ICDs has been strengthened by the discovery that many people with Parkinson's disease have a much higher prevalence of ICDs than do individuals who are unaffected by the illness. Parkinson's is a brain disorder that leads to uncontrollable tremors in the hands, arms, and legs, as well as problems with balance and coordination. The disease develops when dopamine-producing neurons are slowly destroyed, rendering them unable to communicate properly with the part of the brain that controls movement. To treat this deficiency, many Parkinson's patients take dopamine agonists, which are medications that increase dopamine function.

According to Andrew Siderowf of the National Parkinson Foundation, treatment with these drugs is a major risk factor for ICDs, as he writes: "15% of patients treated with a dopamine agonist could have an ICD problem, compared to about 5% who are not receiving a dopamine agonist."[40] A study published in May 2010 found that Parkinson's patients who were taking dopamine agonists were affected by ICDs at two to three times the rate of those who were not taking the medications. These sorts of findings have motivated scientists to further study the relationship between dopamine and ICDs, and research to explore this connection is ongoing.

Genetics and Environment

Many illnesses, including ICDs, tend to run in families, which is a strong indication that these disorders are influenced by genetics. Although few studies have examined the connection between genes and ICDs, some research shows that ICD patients often have a first-degree relative (parent or sibling) who also has the disorder. One of these studies, cited in a September 2010 paper, found that nearly 30 percent of pathological gamblers had a first-degree relative with symptoms of problematic gambling.

In their book *Synopsis of Psychiatry*, Benjamin James Sadock and Virginia Alcott Sadock explore the connection between heredity and intermittent explosive disorder. After extensive research, one of their conclusions was that this disorder is much more common among those with first-degree relatives who also suffer from it. But genetics alone cannot explain why someone has intermittent explosive disorder—or for that matter, any ICD—because the majority of people who are biologically vulnerable do not develop it. Thus, environmental factors also must play a role. For instance, research has shown that most people with intermittent explosive disorder grew up in families where violence was the norm and verbal and physical abuse was common. The Sadocks write: "An unfavorable childhood environment often filled with alcohol dependence, beatings, and threats to life is usual in these patients."[41]

> When referring to biological and environmental factors working together in the development of ICDs, mental health specialists often use a metaphor: Biology loads the gun, and environment pulls the trigger.

According to Elizabeth Corsale, who cofounded the Pathways Institute for Impulse Control along with Smithstein, one environmental factor that is common among those with kleptomania is overwhelming stress. She explains: "We know that impulse disorders are made worse if there is an increase of stress in an individual's life. If you do not suffer from an impulse disorder and you turn the knob up to high stress you are likely to be more impulsive while the stress is high, although unlike a person with impulse disorders you won't keep repeating that impulsive cycle once the stress has lessened." Corsale's experience as a psychologist has taught her that most people who suffer from kleptomania have endured extreme stress in their lives, as she explains: "These stressors may be internal or external and can occur at any stage of life."[42]

> As ICDs continue to be studied, what causes them may some-day be less of a mystery and more of a cer-tainty—and that day cannot come soon enough for those who suffer from the disorders.

Terrence Shulman is convinced that stress played a pivotal role in his development of kleptomania. His first experience with stealing was when he was 10 years old and stole a piece of candy. Shulman's parents were in the process of divorce at the time, and he was overwhelmed by intense feelings of anger, loss, and anxiety. He also felt a great deal of pressure because even at his young age, he was expected to take on additional responsibilities in his father's absence. He explains: "I became the man of the house and assumed the role of helper, which put a lot of pressure on me." Within a few years of his parents' breakup, Shulman was stealing on a regular basis, as he explains: "Shoplifting became my secret outlet to express my pain and symbolically try to get back what I felt I lost, my childhood, my family, myself."[43]

"You Can't Put the Brakes On"

When referring to biological and environmental factors working together in the development of ICDs, mental health specialists often use a metaphor: Biology loads the gun, and environment pulls the trigger. For people who are genetically predisposed to pathological gambling, common triggers include the close proximity of casinos, easy access to gambling on the Internet, and flashy advertising of state lotteries and their multimillion-dollar jackpots. In the case of someone who is biologically vulnerable to compulsive buying, triggers are virtually everywhere, from prolific (and attractive) credit card offers to "irresistible" bargains at shopping malls and with online retailers. Says Bonny Forrest, a psychologist from San Diego: "Think of a car's brakes. If you don't have brake fluid you can't stop. With the impulse to gamble, drink, shop, you can't put the brakes on."[44]

The inability to "put the brakes on" (meaning to resist environmental triggers) is a key component of ICDs, and it is what mental health specialists say makes the disorders so much like substance addictions. In the same way that addicts drink alcohol or take drugs to numb their emotional pain or cope with unbearable stress, ICD sufferers turn to harmful behaviors for relief. For this reason, a growing number of experts are referring to ICDs as behavioral addictions. Speaking of pathological gamblers, the National Council on Problem Gambling writes: "Although no substance is ingested, the problem gambler gets the same effect from gambling as someone else might get from taking a tranquilizer or having a drink. The gambling alters the person's mood and the gambler keeps repeating the behavior attempting to achieve that same effect."[45] The group adds, however, that the person soon needs more and more of the gambling experience to achieve the same emotional effect as before. Thus, he or she develops a tolerance for the behavior just as an alcoholic develops a tolerance for alcohol. Says the National Council on Problem Gambling: "This creates an increased craving for the activity and the gambler finds they have less and less ability to resist as the craving grows in intensity and frequency."[46]

Theories, Not Certainties

For someone whose life is dominated by uncontrollable impulses, hearing that the cause is unknown can be terribly frustrating. But as much as scientists have studied ICDs, they can only make educated guesses about why some people develop them while most do not. Research suggests a variety of factors working together, such as heredity, brain chemistry, and environmental triggers. As ICDs continue to be studied, what causes them may someday be less of a mystery and more of a certainty—and that day cannot come soon enough for those who suffer from the disorders.

What Causes Impulse Control Disorders?

66 Imaging studies of the brain show neurological changes that are present in the brain of an individual who has an impulse control disorder. 99

—Deborah Bauers, "Intermittent Explosive Disorder: Symptoms and Treatments," Helium, May 25, 2010. www.helium.com.

Bauers is a licensed professional counselor from Monument, Colorado.

....

66 Risk factors for ICDs include younger age, smoking and a family history of gambling problems. Neuropsychological factors associated with ICDs include greater depression and anxiety, obsessive-compulsive symptoms, higher novelty seeking and impulsivity. 99

—Andrew Siderowf, "What Are Impulse Control Disorders in PD Patients and Why Is This Important?," National Parkinson Foundation, April 28, 2011. www.parkinson.org.

Siderowf is the medical director of the National Parkinson Foundation Center of Excellence at the University of Pennsylvania Parkinson's Disease and Movement Disorders Center.

....

* Editor's Note: While the definition of a primary source can be narrowly or broadly defined, for the purposes of Compact Research, a primary source consists of: 1) results of original research presented by an organization or researcher; 2) eyewitness accounts of events, personal experience, or work experience; 3) first-person editorials offering pundits' opinions; 4) government officials presenting political plans and/or policies; 5) representatives of organizations presenting testimony or policy.

❝Kleptomania may be linked to problems with a naturally occurring brain chemical (neurotransmitter) called serotonin.❞

—Mayo Clinic, "Kleptomania," October 5, 2011. www.mayoclinic.com.

The Mayo Clinic is a world-renowned medical care facility headquartered in Rochester, Minnesota.

❝The possibility of reaching sexual gratification by a mouse click from home has reduced the social barriers against the use of pornography . . . and has increased the proportion of people feeling a strong demand for regular consumption in an addictive manner.❞

—Peer Briken, Andreas Hill, and Wolfgang Berner, "Hypersexuality: Clinical Aspects," in *Impulse Control Disorders*, Elias Aboujaoude and Lorrin M. Koran, eds. New York: Cambridge University Press, 2010.

Briken, Hill, and Berner are with the Institute of Sex Research and Forensic Psychiatry in Hamburg, Germany.

❝The exact causes of skin picking disorder are unknown. It may be that both biological and environmental factors play a role.❞

—Jeanne M. Fama, "Skin Picking Disorder Fact Sheet," International OCD Foundation, 2010. www.ocfoundation.org.

Fama is a clinical psychologist at Massachusetts General Hospital.

❝Sometimes, hair pulling can be triggered by a stressful event such as a change of schools, abuse, family conflict or trauma. In other cases, changing hormones associated with puberty may trigger symptoms.❞

—Paul Latimer, "Trichotillomania," Castanet, July 27, 2011. www.castanet.net.

Latimer is a psychiatrist, medical researcher, and writer from British Columbia, Canada.

❝For the most part, anger disorders cannot be blamed on bad neurology, genes or biochemistry. They arise from a failure to recognize and consciously address anger as it arises, before it becomes pathological and dangerous, starting in childhood.❞

—Stephen A. Diamond, "Anger Disorder: What It Is and What We Can Do About It," *Psychology Today*, April 3, 2009. www.psychologytoday.com.

Diamond is a clinical and forensic psychologist from Los Angeles, California.

❝When contemplating why people gamble, it is important to understand that there is usually no one specific cause for pathological gambling.❞

—Roxanne Dryden-Edwards, "Gambling Addiction (Compulsive or Pathological Gambling)," MedicineNet, April 7, 2010. www.medicinenet.com.

Dryden-Edwards is a psychiatrist from Montgomery County, Maryland.

❝Kleptomania developing after head trauma has been reported in the literature.❞

—Farid Ramzi Talih, "Kleptomania and Potential Exacerbating Factors," *Innovations in Clinical Neuroscience*, October 2011. www.ncbi.nlm.nih.gov.

Talih is director of psychiatry and codirector of Sleep Medicine at the Ashtabula County Medical Center in Ashtabula, Ohio.

❝As with many other disorders, trichotillomania may develop due to a combination of genetic, hormonal, emotional (family stress, for example) and environmental factors.❞

—Trichotillomania Learning Center, "About Trichotillomania," 2011. www.trich.org.

The Trichotillomania Learning Center is devoted to research and providing support and services to those who suffer from trichotillomania.

Facts and Illustrations

What Causes Impulse Control Disorders?

- According to researchers from New York's Rockefeller University, studies with twins have found that about **45 percent** of ICD cases are accounted for by genetic factors.

- According to psychiatrist and ICD expert Jon E. Grant, growing data suggest that **multiple neurotransmitter systems** are involved in the development of ICDs.

- In a February 2011 paper, psychiatrists from the Impulse Control Disorders Clinic at the University of Minnesota cite a study that found that **56.5 percent** of pathological gamblers had at least one first-degree relative with alcohol dependence and 26.9 percent had a first-degree relative with gambling problems.

- According to the Mayo Clinic, people who **abuse drugs or alcohol** have a markedly increased risk of developing intermittent explosive disorder.

- A 2010 study of 3,090 individuals with Parkinson's disease found that nearly **14 percent** suffered from at least one ICD, which was attributed to medications known as dopamine agonists.

- According to the Institute of Sex Research and Forensic Psychiatry in Hamburg, Germany, **testosterone levels in men** may be associated with aggression and violent behavior, which are characteristics of intermittent explosive disorder.

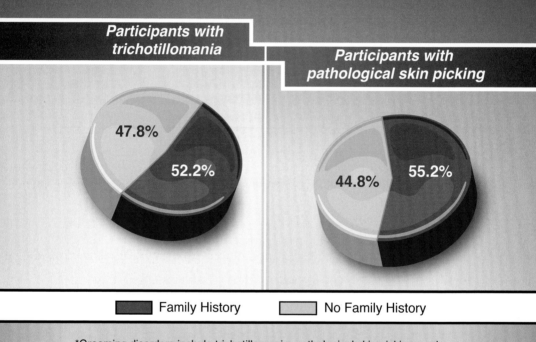

Grooming Disorders and Genetics

Although scientists do not know exactly what causes impulse control disorders, many believe that heredity is a factor. A study published in 2010, which involved 70 patients with trichotillomania and 59 with pathological skin picking, found that over half of the participants had a family history of grooming disorders,* as these charts illustrate.

Participants with trichotillomania

47.8%

52.2%

Participants with pathological skin picking

44.8%

55.2%

■ Family History   □ No Family History

*Grooming disorders include trichotillomania, pathological skin picking, and onychophagia (compulsive nail biting).

Source: Brian L. Odlaug, Suck Won Kim, and Jon E. Grant, "Quality of Life and Clinical Severity in Pathological Skin Picking and Trichotillomania," *Journal of Anxiety Disorders*, December 2010, pp. 823–29.

- Elias Aboujaoude, director of the Impulse Control Disorders Clinic at Stanford University School of Medicine, says that the Internet is a particularly dangerous trigger for compulsive buyers because **spending money online** can distort their reality of how much is actually being spent.

Risk Factors for Intermittent Explosive Disorder

No one knows why some people suffer from intermittent explosive disorder (IED), which involves aggressive outbursts of rage that are often violent and unprovoked. Scientists have identified a number of risk factors that could work together in the development of the disorder.

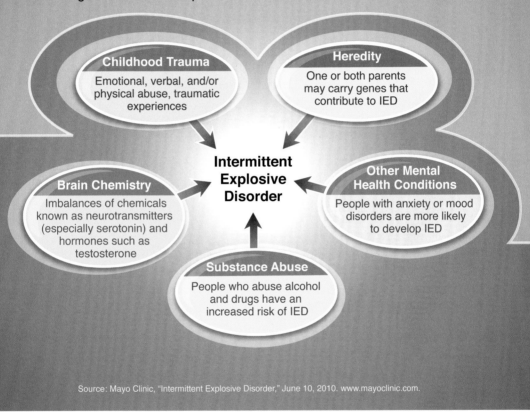

Childhood Trauma
Emotional, verbal, and/or physical abuse, traumatic experiences

Heredity
One or both parents may carry genes that contribute to IED

Intermittent Explosive Disorder

Brain Chemistry
Imbalances of chemicals known as neurotransmitters (especially serotonin) and hormones such as testosterone

Other Mental Health Conditions
People with anxiety or mood disorders are more likely to develop IED

Substance Abuse
People who abuse alcohol and drugs have an increased risk of IED

Source: Mayo Clinic, "Intermittent Explosive Disorder," June 10, 2010. www.mayoclinic.com.

- In a May 2011 online poll by the Shulman Center for Compulsive Theft, Spending & Hoarding, nearly **40 percent** of respondents blamed childhood abuse for their compulsive stealing.

- A paper published in August 2011 by researchers from Turkey states that children who exhibit high levels of **aggressiveness**, are shy, and are rejected by their peers have a markedly higher likelihood of being involved in fire setting than children without these qualities.

What Are the Effects of Impulse Control Disorders?

66Impulse-control disorders such as pathological gambling, sexual addiction, and compulsive shopping cause enormous suffering in people's lives.99

—Robert Miller, a psychologist from San Marino, California.

66ICDs can have substantial financial and social consequences. Many patients act on their impulses in secret because they are aware that the behaviors are socially inappropriate.99

—Andrew Siderowf, medical director of the National Parkinson Foundation Center of Excellence at the University of Pennsylvania Parkinson's Disease and Movement Disorders Center.

W hen Brittney Matheson (not her real name) first started shoplifting as a teenager, she considered her actions an expression of anger toward mega-retailers such as Walmart. She vowed never to steal from small businesses, but within a year had broken that vow and could not leave any store without stealing something. "The scary part was that I couldn't stop," she says, "and I had no idea why."[47] Matheson continued shoplifting on a regular basis and always managed to get away with it—until the day a security guard caught her with a knapsack filled with items she had lifted off the store's shelves.

Matheson was terrified as she listened to the man's warnings about the consequences of being arrested and having a criminal record. When the security guard finished speaking, Matheson was shocked that he let her go without calling the police. He told her that she seemed like a good person who had made a mistake, but little did he know that she had actually stolen over $6,000 worth of merchandise over the previous three years. The experience frightened Matheson into realizing that she had a serious problem and needed help before she ruined her future.

Emotional Turmoil

People with ICDs often live in a state of uncertainty, fear, and shame. Unlike some mental illnesses that involve losing touch with reality, most ICD sufferers are well aware that their behaviors are not normal, but they cannot control their overwhelming impulses. Referring to the turmoil associated with trichotillomania, psychiatrist and medical researcher Paul Latimer writes: "Far from enjoying the experience, individuals with this condition feel significant distress about their behaviour and also experience difficulties in social, work and other areas of their lives as a result. Many people with trichotillomania avoid intimate relationships and try to hide their hair pulling behaviour."[48]

A teenager named Maddie has been pulling her hair out since she was nine years old, and she describes living with trichotillomania as "an ongoing battle every day, all day." When her hair became noticeably thin, her mother began to criticize her, saying that she should just stop pulling it. Says Maddie: "She made it seem like I could be just another *quick fix* like the chores she has people do around the house—as if stopping pulling could be just as easy as changing a light bulb."[49] Along with feeling bad because of her mother's lack of understanding, Maddie was deeply ashamed of how she looked. Since elementary school she had not left home without wearing a hat so

> " Unlike some mental illnesses that involve losing touch with reality, most ICD sufferers are well aware that their behaviors are not normal, but they cannot control their overwhelming impulses. "

no one could see how much of her hair was gone. "I felt like a freak and a sick person," she says, "and not even my mom could understand me. She accused me of 'not trying hard enough.' But that was so wrong. I tried really hard . . . but even when I did I felt like I could never stop pulling no matter how hard I tried."[50]

Pathological skin picking can be every bit as hard for sufferers to stop—and cause just as much anxiety and embarrassment. Boston psychologist Jeanne M. Fama explains: "Skin picking disorder can hurt a person emotionally, physically, and socially. In addition to feeling shame and embarrassment, people with skin picking disorder can have other psychological problems like depression and anxiety." Fama adds that skin picking can cause physical problems such as severe pain during and after picking, sores covering the skin, permanent scarring, and infections. "In extreme cases," she says, "skin picking can cause sores severe enough to require surgery."[51]

> **Rather than pull out their hair, pick their skin, steal, or gamble, compulsive shoppers feel a desperate need to buy things.**

A young woman named Annie has picked her skin so much that she has been hospitalized multiple times for infection. Showers are painful because the water hurts her sores, and she has to be careful what clothes she wears because lint gets into the sores and infects them. Her body is seriously disfigured from the picking, as she explains: "My skin, my body is scarred from head to toe. I've destroyed every inch of my body." But the worst part, says Annie, is not the pain or the scars but how isolated and alone she feels. She explains: "It's a very lonely thing to deal with. It's very shameful; you feel embarrassed and people judge you because you look different and they just don't understand, because what grown woman mutilates her whole body?"[52]

"Just Like Being a Junkie"

Like all ICDs, compulsive buying starts with tension that builds until it becomes overpowering. Rather than pull out their hair, pick their skin, steal, or gamble, compulsive shoppers feel a desperate need to buy things.

These are often items they do not need, or even necessarily want, but compulsive buying is not about needs or wants. It stems from urges that are impossible to ignore, even if it means draining a savings account, racking up thousands of dollars in debt, and destroying relationships. Says University of Iowa psychiatry professor Donald W. Black: "Usually, the idea is, 'I see it, I like it, I want it, I'll buy it—and damn the consequences."[53] As is typical of people with ICDs, compulsive buyers feel a rush of pleasure after a shopping spree. The thrill fades fast, though, and is soon replaced by regret, guilt, and fears about being unable to stop.

Rachel Diaz knows from personal experience the extreme highs and lows of being a compulsive buyer. Unhappy in her marriage and stressed out from a high-pressure sales job, she turned to shopping as a source of relief. Diaz says it was the one thing that made her feel empowered when so much about her life was going wrong. She writes: "I somehow felt that if I bought the outfit from the happy window scene, that I might be happy myself. But then things got out of hand pretty quickly."[54]

At one point Diaz was spending $1,200 per month on clothes and had accumulated 150 pairs of shoes, 35 purses, and 25 pairs of sunglasses. Her walk-in closet was stuffed with clothes with the tags still attached, yet she could not stop shopping for more. She went out of her way to hide the merchandise from her husband, stuffing it in the trunk of her car or the back of her closet. Although she could not keep from returning to the stores over and over again, she felt ashamed and embarrassed, knowing that the salespeople recognized her and were likely wondering what her problem was. "It's just like being a junkie," she says. "You want the fix, but you don't want to get caught."[55]

Reviled by Society

Along with being harmful to sufferers and to those closest to them, some ICDs are associated with criminal acts—and society is neither tolerant of nor sympathetic toward people who commit such crimes. This is particularly true of intermittent explosive disorder, which involves aggressive outbursts of anger that often lead to violence. The degree of blame that sufferers should be held accountable for is debated by mental health experts. According to therapist Deborah Bauers, the disorder is not typically viewed as grounds for mental incapacity when someone commits a violent crime, as she writes: "While Intermittent Explosive Disorder is a psychiatric disorder and should be treated accordingly, episodes of violent behavior frequently become criminal in nature and can lead to incarceration. . . . As the saying goes, 'you do the crime; you do the time.'"[56]

Although it was highly controversial, the defense of intermittent explosive disorder saved Bradley Waldroup from being sentenced to the death penalty in 2010. In a fit of blinding rage four years before, Waldroup had shot his wife's friend to death, and then almost killed his wife by ruthlessly hacking her with a machete. His defense team said there was no question that Waldroup had committed the crimes. They argued that his actions were not premeditated, however. Rather, they blamed his mental illness for the rage that led to the attack. "It wasn't a *who done it?*" says defense attorney Wylie Richardson. "It was a *why done it?*"[57]

> "Along with being harmful to sufferers and to those closest to them, some ICDs are associated with criminal acts—and society is neither tolerant of nor sympathetic toward people who commit such crimes."

A blood test proved that Waldroup had a rare genetic abnormality known as the "warrior gene," named after its association with violent tendencies. The defense attorneys argued that this abnormality, along with a history of abuse as a child, resulted in the development of intermittent explosive disorder and explained his deadly rampage. Prosecutors, on the other hand, argued that Waldroup was a cold-blooded killer who deserved to die for his actions. The jury agreed with the defense that Waldroup was mentally ill and not entirely responsible for his actions. He was found guilty of voluntary manslaughter, rather than murder, which meant that he was not eligible for the death penalty.

"Never Enough"

Mental health professionals say that pathological gambling is among the most devastating of all ICDs. Those who have the disorder gamble away not only their money but also their careers, their families, their friends, and often their futures. Laura M. Letson of the New York Council on

Problem Gambling writes: "Numerous costs of pathological gambling cannot be quantified, such as the emotional pain associated with bankruptcy, divorce, neglect, and related difficulties experienced by gamblers and others in their lives."[58] The inevitable regret, grief, and shame can fill pathological gamblers with such anguish that they decide life is no longer worth living—and the high suicide rate is evidence of that. According to the National Council on Problem Gambling, approximately 20 percent of pathological gamblers attempt suicide.

Michael J. Burke came perilously close to being included in that statistic. Formerly a successful attorney from Howell, Michigan, Burke's experience with gambling had been limited to bets on poker games with his buddies and yearly trips to Las Vegas with his wife. That changed, however, when a new casino opened in Windsor, Canada, less than an hour's drive from his home. Before long, Burke was heading to Windsor several times a week, lying about his whereabouts, and gambling with increasingly larger amounts of money. He won big and he lost big, which led to desperate—as well as dishonest—ways of getting more gambling money. He cleaned out his daughters' college fund, forged his wife's name on a $200,000 mortgage, and began making unauthorized withdrawals from his clients' accounts. Says Burke: "Gamblers will do anything they can to get money to gamble."[59]

Burke reached rock bottom one night in September 2000. Overcome with self-loathing and despair, he sat alone in his office, held a gun to his temple, and prepared to pull the trigger— then had a sudden change of heart and put the weapon down. Six months later he turned himself in to the state attorney general's office, was arraigned and indicted for embezzlement, and spent three years in prison. Today Burke still owes $1.6 million to the victims of his crimes, which he is paying with the proceeds from a book he wrote about his experiences as a pathological

> **The inevitable regret, grief, and shame can fill pathological gamblers with such anguish that they decide life is no longer worth living—and the high suicide rate is evidence of that.**

gambler. In the book, Burke recounts the comments of a casino host who once "leaned over my shoulder and whispered in my ear, 'Remember, Burke, it's never enough.' He had uttered the single greatest truth shared by all addicts."[60]

A Tough Way to Live

Depending on which disorder they have, people who suffer from ICDs experience everything from deep emotional pain to physical disfigurement, financial devastation, and society's intolerance and scorn. No matter how badly they may want to be free from their dysfunctional behaviors, they feel like their lives have been hijacked by impulses too overpowering to control. Unable to resist the urges, they perform the harmful behaviors, feel the usual sense of euphoria, and then suffer the inevitable letdown—and the vicious cycle repeats itself over and over again.

Primary Source Quotes*

What Are the Effects of Impulse Control Disorders?

66 By their very nature, some impulse control disorders can result in illegal or criminal behavior. 99

—Amitabh Saha, "A Case of Intermittent Explosive Disorder," *Industrial Psychology Journal*, March 16, 2011. www.industrialpsychiatry.org.

Saha is a psychiatrist from Jodhpur, India.

66 People with impulse control disorder symptoms often feel as though their lives are out of control and they have limited ability to respond in healthy and safe ways to stress and anxiety. 99

—Nicole Stelter, "Impulse Control Disorder Symptoms," Livestrong, May 4, 2011. www.livestrong.com.

Stelter is a psychologist from Cypress, California.

* Editor's Note: While the definition of a primary source can be narrowly or broadly defined, for the purposes of Compact Research, a primary source consists of: 1) results of original research presented by an organization or researcher; 2) eyewitness accounts of events, personal experience, or work experience; 3) first-person editorials offering pundits' opinions; 4) government officials presenting political plans and/or policies; 5) representatives of organizations presenting testimony or policy.

❝Pathological gamblers have the highest rate of suicidal ideation and attempts among persons suffering from addictive disorders.❞

—Laura M. Letson, "Pathological Gambling: Promoting Risk, Provoking Ruin," in *Impulse Control Disorders*, Elias Aboujaoude and Lorrin M. Koran, eds. New York: Cambridge University Press, 2010.

Letson is with the New York Council on Problem Gambling.

❝Kleptomania is an impulse control disorder that can cause significant impairment and serious consequences.❞

—Farid Ramzi Talih, "Kleptomania and Potential Exacerbating Factors," *Innovations in Clinical Neuroscience*, October 2011. www.ncbi.nlm.nih.gov.

Talih is director of psychiatry and codirector of Sleep Medicine at the Ashtabula County Medical Center in Ashtabula, Ohio.

❝Though most of the time hair pulling and skin picking aren't life-threatening, they can be. Ingesting hair leads to emergency abdominal surgery. Despair over pulling or picking contributes to suicidal depression.❞

—Jennifer Raikes, "Is Trich Another Bourgeois Problem?," *TLC Blog*, August 29, 2011. http://blog.trich.org.

Raikes is executive director of the Trichotillomania Learning Center.

❝Most pyromania subjects who are arrested are judged to be criminals and are condemned to jail sentences rather than managed via psychiatric care.❞

—Candice Germain and Michel Lejoyeux, "Pyromania: Clinical Aspects," in *Impulse Control Disorders*, ed. Elias Aboujaoude and Lorrin M. Koran. New York: Cambridge University Press, 2010.

Germain and Lejoyeux are psychiatrists from France.

"Skin picking disorder can also interfere with social life, school, and/or work. Mild to severe pain during or after picking; sores, scars, disfigurement; and other medical problems like infections can also occur."

—Jeanne M. Fama, "Skin Picking Disorder Fact Sheet," International OCD Foundation, 2010. www.ocfoundation.org.

Fama is a clinical psychologist at Massachusetts General Hospital.

"A person who has [intermittent explosive disorder] is like a stick of dynamite with a very short fuse. His explosive behaviors can occur with little provocation which makes living with him a frightening proposition."

—Deborah Bauers, "Intermittent Explosive Disorder: Symptoms and Treatments," Helium, May 25, 2010. www.helium.com.

Bauers is a licensed professional counselor from Monument, Colorado.

"Left untreated, kleptomania can result in severe emotional, legal and financial problems. . . . Because you know stealing is wrong but you feel powerless to resist the impulse, you may be wracked by guilt, shame, self-loathing and humiliation. You may otherwise lead a moral, upstanding life and be confused and upset by your compulsive stealing."

—Mayo Clinic, "Kleptomania," October 5, 2011. www.mayoclinic.com.

The Mayo Clinic is a world-renowned medical care facility headquartered in Rochester, Minnesota.

Facts and Illustrations

What Are the Effects of Impulse Control Disorders?

- A study published in December 2009 involved 100 people with kleptomania, of whom **68.3 percent** had been arrested. Of those, 36.6 percent had not been convicted, 20.8 percent had been convicted and incarcerated, and 10.9 percent had been convicted but not incarcerated.

- The Trichotillomania Learning Center states that **fear of exposure** leads many trichotillomania sufferers to avoid medical and dental care.

- The Mayo Clinic states that people with trichotillomania who eat the hair they pull out can develop large, **matted hairballs** in their digestive tract, which can lead to vomiting, intestinal obstruction, and even death.

- New York psychologist April Lane Benson estimates that between **one-third and one-half** of compulsive buyers eventually develop hoarding disorder.

- According to the Institute of Sex Research and Forensic Psychiatry in Hamburg, Germany, **hypersexuality** carries a higher-than-normal risk of sexually transmitted diseases.

- A study by ICD experts Brian L. Odlaug and Jon E. Grant found that sores on the skin, scarring, and infections were common among people suffering from **pathological skin picking**.

The Disastrous Consequences of Pathological Gambling

Mental health professionals widely agree that pathological gambling is one of the most devastating impulse control disorders in terms of its effects on the gambler, his or her family, and society. Some of the most common adverse effects are shown here.

Financial	Enormous debt, ruined credit, home foreclosure, bankruptcy; estimated annual costs to society is $5 billion.
Impact on family	Emotional pain associated with bankruptcy, divorce, and neglect; children of pathological gamblers often develop high levels of risk-taking behaviors.
Employment and productivity loss	Preoccupation with gambling can result in poor job performance, absenteeism, health problems, job loss, and unemployment; research has shown that pathological gamblers are more than four times as likely as low-risk gamblers to have lost a job and over three times as likely to have been fired.
Crime/Legal problems	Pathological gamblers often resort to crime (such as embezzlement) to finance bets, replace losses, or pay off gambling debts, bookies, or others; arrests and imprisonment are common among pathological gamblers.
Suicide risk	According to the National Council on Problem Gambling, pathological gamblers have the highest rate of suicidal thoughts and attempts among all individuals with addictive disorders; about 20 percent of pathological gamblers attempt suicide.

Source: Laura M. Letson, "Pathological Gambling: Promoting Risk, Provoking Ruin," in *Impulse Control Disorders*, Elias Aboujaoude and Lorrin M. Koran, eds. New York: Cambridge University Press, 2010. pp. 76–79.

- The California statute that prohibits employment discrimination on the basis of **physical or mental disability** does not apply to kleptomania, pyromania, compulsive gambling, or sexual behavior disorders.

Poor Self-Esteem Biggest Problem for Kleptomaniacs

In a May 2011 survey by the Shulman Center for Compulsive Theft, Spending & Hoarding, participants, the majority of whom were women, revealed how kleptomania had negatively affected their lives.

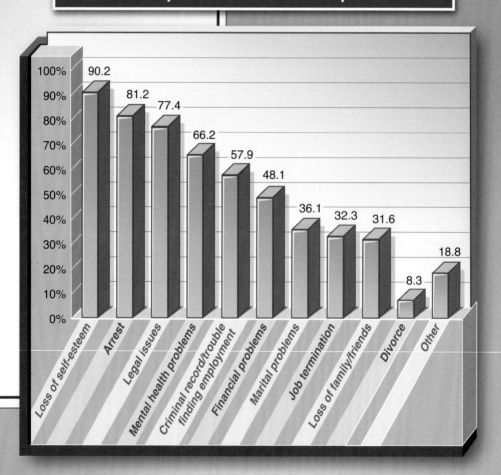

Percent of respondents who have experienced . . .

Category	Percent
Loss of self-esteem	90.2
Arrest	81.2
Legal issues	77.4
Mental health problems	66.2
Criminal record/trouble finding employment	57.9
Financial problems	48.1
Marital problems	36.1
Job termination	32.3
Loss of family/friends	31.6
Divorce	8.3
Other	18.8

Note: Participants could choose multiple categories.

Source: Shulman Center for Compulsive Theft, Spending & Hoarding, "Theft/Recovery Survey," May 2011. www.theshulmancenter.com.

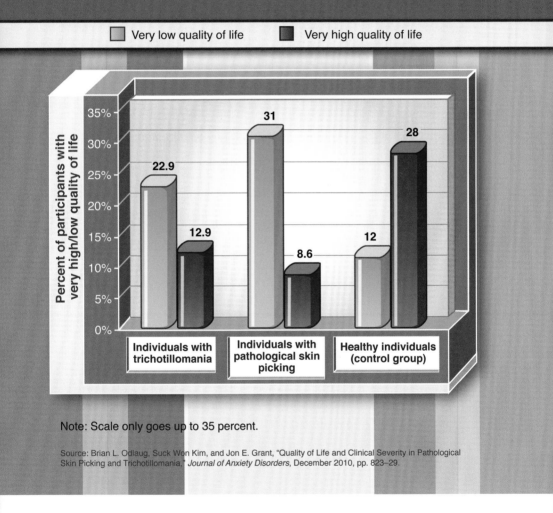

Trichotillomania and Skin Picking Impair Quality of Life

For a study published in December 2010, researchers from the University of Minnesota's Impulse Control Disorders Clinic evaluated the quality of life of people suffering from either trichotillomania or pathological skin picking. As this graph shows, those with the disorders had a much more negative perception of their quality of life than did healthy participants.

Very low quality of life   Very high quality of life

Percent of participants with very high/low quality of life

22.9
12.9
31
8.6
12
28

Individuals with trichotillomania

Individuals with pathological skin picking

Healthy individuals (control group)

Note: Scale only goes up to 35 percent.

Source: Brian L. Odlaug, Suck Won Kim, and Jon E. Grant, "Quality of Life and Clinical Severity in Pathological Skin Picking and Trichotillomania," *Journal of Anxiety Disorders*, December 2010, pp. 823–29.

- According to the Canada Safety Council, at least 200 problem gamblers in Canada **commit suicide** each year.

- A May 2011 online poll by the Shulman Center for Compulsive Theft, Spending & Hoarding found that over **50 percent** of respondents had served time in jail for stealing.

- According to the mental health and addiction website ChooseHelp, teenagers who become problem gamblers have **higher rates of drug and alcohol abuse**, risky sexual behaviors, violent acts, mental illness, and school and family problems.

- In a May 2011 online poll by the Shulman Center for Compulsive Theft, Spending & Hoarding, **36 percent** of respondents said they had experienced marital problems as a result of their stealing, and over 8 percent were divorced.

- According to former attorney and recovered pathological gambler Michael J. Burke, **two out of three compulsive gamblers** commit an illegal act to obtain money for gambling.

Can People Overcome Impulse Control Disorders?

> **"**Although ICDs often are severely disabling and embarrassing, there is help and hope. Treatments are available, and ongoing research continues to promise newer and better options for people to control these behaviors.**"**
>
> —Jon E. Grant, a psychiatrist who codirects the Impulse Control Disorders Clinic at the University of Minnesota and who is an expert on ICDs.

> **"**Nowhere is the therapeutic alliance more important than in the work therapists do with people who have impulse-control disorders.**"**
>
> —Linda Seligman and Lourie W. Reichenberg, coauthors of the book *Selecting Effective Treatments*.

Mental health professionals who treat patients with ICDs are the first to acknowledge that the disorders can be extremely tough to overcome. One of the biggest hurdles is that most people who suffer from them never reach out for help. Often they are ashamed of their impulsive behaviors and want to keep them hidden, or they have no idea that their disorder is treatable, or both. Many with kleptomania are frightened that if they confess to stealing, they will be arrested and jailed. As recovered sufferer Shelley explains: "Where do you go [for help] when you're engaging in criminal behavior?"[61] Those who compulsively pick at their skin or pull out their hair typically isolate themselves, convinced that no one would ever understand them, much less be able to help them recover. Pathological gamblers are often reluctant to seek treatment because it would mean giving up the one activity that relieves their overpowering tension—even if that activity is destroying their lives.

> **Pathological gamblers are often reluctant to seek treatment because it would mean giving up the one activity that relieves their overpowering tension—even if that activity is destroying their lives.**

Once someone has worked up the courage to seek professional help, he or she must be willing to face whatever problems exist and accept that overcoming the disorder requires a great deal of time, effort, and commitment. Psychologist Elizabeth Corsale explains: "Treatment takes a long time; there are no quick fixes."[62] Corsale adds that an essential part of ICD treatment is getting at the root of what caused it, since compulsive behaviors (such as stealing) are often symptoms of deeper psychological problems. "We humans create a psychology of meaning as it relates to the context of our life and our unique differences that make us who we are," says Corsale. "This has to be included in the treatment, particularly treatment that involves relapse prevention. Treatment can't ever be one size fits all."[63]

The Value of Therapy

Therapy is widely considered to be an essential part of recovery from ICDs, but the kind of therapy depends on the specific disorder. One type that has been effective for people with trichotillomania is called habit reversal training, which involves helping patients learn how to recognize situations that lead to hair pulling and to substitute other behaviors in its place. For example, a therapist might suggest that when the pulling urge becomes strong, patients clench their fists to "freeze" the urge or that they purposely redirect their hands away from their hair and touch an ear instead. The Mayo Clinic writes: "Sometimes elements of other therapies may be blended with habit reversal training. For instance, your care provider may use cognitive therapy to help you challenge and examine distorted beliefs you may have in relation to hair pulling."[64]

Cognitive behavioral therapy (CBT) is one of the most frequently recommended therapies for patients who suffer from ICDs. It focuses on identifying unhealthy, negative, and irrational beliefs and understanding that the beliefs are at the root of problems such as uncontrollable impulses. According to the authors of the book *Overcoming Impulse Control Problems*, CBT is based on the theory that feelings and behaviors are caused by the patient's own thoughts, rather than resulting from situations, events, or other people. They write: "CBT is structured and goal oriented, with the therapeutic goal of helping you unlearn your unwanted reactions and learn a new way of reacting."[65]

According to an April 2011 article in the *Harvard Mental Health Letter*, CBT is a promising type of therapy for people with intermittent explosive disorder—one of the most difficult ICDs to treat. The authors reference a study by researchers from the University of Chicago, which involved a small group of patients who suffered from the disorder. Some of them participated in either group or individual CBT sessions, while the rest made up the control group and underwent no therapy. At the end of 12 weeks, all CBT participants had significant reductions in aggressive feelings and anger and were less depressed than the control group participants. The biggest improvement was observed in those enrolled in individual CBT sessions, who, according to the article's authors, "also reported an improvement in their overall quality of life. Three months later, the improvements persisted."[66]

> "Cognitive behavioral therapy (CBT) is one of the most frequently recommended therapies for patients who suffer from ICDs."

Another ICD that has proved to respond well to CBT is compulsive buying disorder. Once patients have identified the psychological issues that lead to their excessive shopping, they learn to compensate by intentionally substituting other feelings and behaviors. One person who recovered from compulsive buying disorder was Brian Kearney, a college student from Rockaway, New Jersey. By the time Kearney finally realized how serious his problem was, he was spending over $1,500 per month on designer clothes and expensive gifts for his friends. Therapy helped him realize that his problem was rooted in feelings of inferiority, as he explains: "Buying $300 jeans, I felt better than everybody else." As his therapy progressed, Kearney went through what he calls a "journey of self-discovery," during which he came to see that shopping was a dysfunctional, unhealthy way of attempting to cope with his insecurities—and it changed his life. "If I see a pair of $300 jeans now," he says, "I think, 'Why did I want them so bad?' I can feel just as good in sweat pants, and if people are going to judge me on what I'm wearing, then I don't want to know them."[67]

Beneficial Meds

People who suffer from ICDs often benefit from taking prescription medications, usually in conjunction with one or more kinds of therapy. No drugs have been developed specifically for ICDs, but certain types designed to treat other conditions have proved to be effective in a number of cases. One example is a group of antidepressants known as selective serotonin reuptake inhibitors (SSRIs), whose function is to correct serotonin levels in the brain. The Mayo Clinic writes: "Changing the balance of serotonin seems to help brain cells send and receive chemical messages, which in turn boosts mood. SSRIs are called selective because they seem to primarily affect serotonin, not other neurotransmitters."[68] Research has shown that SSRIs are most effective in treating intermittent explosive disorder, pathological skin picking, compulsive buying, and hypersexuality.

Research also suggests success with a different group of drugs known as opioid antagonists. These are designed to block the effects of natural chemicals in the brain known as opioids, thereby reducing urge-related symptoms. One opioid antagonist, naltrexone, is commonly used to diminish cravings felt by people with alcohol or drug addictions. Because it works so well in those situations, researchers tried naltrexone with groups of pathological gamblers. According to a 2011 paper about the study, participants were divided into two groups, with one given naltrexone and the control group given a placebo (a harmless substance that has no effects). In three separate studies the naltrexone groups showed significant decreases in gambling urges and behaviors compared with participants who received placebos. In their paper, the study authors write: "The data regarding the use of opioid antagonists for [pathological gambling] are persuasive and provide the strongest evidence of any medications for the treatment of ICDs."[69]

The same research team conducted naltrexone research with patients suffering from other ICDs, and the results were equally promising. In a study that involved a group of kleptomania sufferers, the naltrexone group showed marked reductions in the urge to steal and in actual stealing behavior. One of the participants was Shelley, who was both thrilled and stunned at the difference the drug made. She says the results were "amazing and immediate," as she explains: "For the first time in my life, my brain knew what it felt like to feel normal. . . . I don't feel so tormented."[70] A similar study involved 17 individuals with trichotillomania, and those who were given naltrexone experienced significant decreases in symptom severity. About half of the participants who took the drug reported a 50 percent decrease in hair-pulling symptoms compared with no progress reported by the placebo group.

> " No drugs have been developed specifically for ICDs, but certain types designed to treat other conditions have proved to be effective in a number of cases. "

Promising Findings

Trichotillomania was also the focus of research published in July 2009 by the University of Minnesota's Impulse Control Disorder Clinic. In this study, rather than treating participants with drugs, the research team gave them an amino acid known as N-acetylcysteine, which laboratory experiments have shown to reduce the cravings of rats addicted to cocaine. The lead researcher says that because of that finding, the team "thought it might be useful for a range of compulsive problems."[71]

After 12 weeks of treatment with a daily dose of N-acetylcysteine, over half of the participants had a considerable reduction in hair pulling. The researchers determined that the substance worked by reducing brain levels of the neurotransmitter glutamate, whose function is to trigger excitement. Researcher Jon E. Grant says that this sends a message of hope to trichotillomania sufferers, as it could someday lead to new treatments for the disorder and perhaps for other ICDs as well. He shares his thoughts: "The encouraging message from this study is that perhaps we are learning more about what is happening in the brains of people who pull their hair and that we can and will have even better treatments down the road."[72]

No Way Out

Coping with an ICD for years can take a heavy toll on sufferers, causing them to feel alone, depressed, and hopeless. Because so many are never diagnosed and treated, the risk of suicide is high—especially for pathological gamblers. This was one of the findings of a study published in September 2010 by researchers from Montreal, Quebec, Canada. Focusing on 122 people who had committed suicide, the team performed psychological autopsies, which involved gathering extensive information from friends and family members of the deceased. The team learned that of those who had suffered from pathological gambling before their deaths, only 2 percent had undergone therapy at any point in their lifetime. Says lead researcher Richard Boyer: "I think health professionals should be more vigilant in looking for signs of suicide among pathological gamblers. The sooner this disorder is diagnosed, the sooner therapy can begin and the better chances for success."[73]

> **Coping with an ICD for years can take a heavy toll on sufferers, causing them to feel alone, depressed, and hopeless.**

One woman who took her own life after struggling with pathological gambling was Yoo Choi of British Columbia, Canada. To most everyone who knew her, Choi appeared to be a happy, fun-loving person, but she had battled a severe gambling problem for years and had run up $100,000 in gambling-related debt. She underwent therapy, but it did not curb her desperate need to gamble. At several casinos she enrolled in voluntary self-exclusion programs, which use facial recognition technology to help staff spot problem gamblers and keep them from entering the premises. But as soon as her exclusion expired,

Choi went back to gambling again. In June 2011 Choi telephoned her husband to apologize for not being able to beat her gambling problem, and then she committed suicide. "It's a wake-up call," her husband says. "If you know someone, be a little bit more aware of the repercussions. It can go, as I found out, beyond rock bottom."[74]

"Ongoing Journey of Change"

As bleak as things may seem to those who suffer from ICDs, treatments are available and have proved to be effective in numerous cases. Therapy can help patients better understand the root of their problems, and medications can work wonders at reducing urges. Most of all, people need to realize that there is always hope, and they should never give up. Psychologist and former kleptomania sufferer Terrence Shulman shares his thoughts: "As a recovering person myself since 1990, I relate to addicts and know the struggles of recovery and peeling back the layers of the onion to get to greater self-awareness. . . . Change is a process. So, as we see, this is why recovery is a one-day-at-a-time, ongoing journey of change."[75]

Primary Source Quotes*

Can People Overcome Impulse Control Disorders?

66 Low levels of serotonin have been associated with several impulse control disorders, and treatment with medications to enhance serotonin levels has appeared to alleviate these disorders in many patients.99

—Letty Workman and David Paper, "Compulsive Buying: A Theoretical Framework," *Journal of Business Inquiry*, 2010. www.uvu.edu.

Workman is a professor at Utah Valley University and Paper is a professor at Utah State University.

66 There is no real cure for kleptomania, but through treatment, medication, and psychotherapy, some are able to control their compulsions and end the cycle of stealing.99

—Dhiren Patel, "How to Deal with a Kleptomaniac," Solace Counseling, April 28, 2011. www.solacecounseling.com.

Patel is a psychologist from Dallas, Texas.

* Editor's Note: While the definition of a primary source can be narrowly or broadly defined, for the purposes of Compact Research, a primary source consists of: 1) results of original research presented by an organization or researcher; 2) eyewitness accounts of events, personal experience, or work experience; 3) first-person editorials offering pundits' opinions; 4) government officials presenting political plans and/or policies; 5) representatives of organizations presenting testimony or policy.

66 **Psychotherapy is necessary in order to get the support, understanding and help you need to work through the issues and problems that self-destructive impulses create in one's life.** 99

—Samantha Smithstein, "Gains and Losses: Helping People Stop Stealing (Who Can't Stop Themselves)," *What The Wild Things Are* (blog), *Psychology Today,* July 15, 2011. www.psychologytoday.com.

Smithstein is a psychologist and cofounder of the Pathways Institute for Impulse Control in San Francisco.

66 **All too often people with kleptomania and compulsive stealing issues are never assessed or treated for their stealing behaviors. Those who seek treatment often arrive in therapy when their criminal records are so dire that they are facing life altering consequences.** 99

—Elizabeth Corsale, "For Richer or Poorer: From Celebrity Compulsive Stealing to the Regular Joe," Pathways Institute for Impulse Control, February 8, 2011. www.pathwaysinstitute.net.

Corsale is a marriage and family therapist and codirector of the Pathways Institute for Impulse Control.

66 **Unfortunately, because many people do not know that there is help for skin picking disorder, many people with the disorder continue to suffer with it.** 99

—Jeanne M. Fama, "Skin Picking Disorder Fact Sheet," International OCD Foundation, 2010. www.ocfoundation.org.

Fama is a clinical psychologist at Massachusetts General Hospital.

66 **Although an exact cause is not fully understood, there are some effective treatments available for trichotillomania. Usually a combination of cognitive behaviour therapy and medication provides the most relief from symptoms.** 99

—Paul Latimer, "Trichotillomania," Castanet, July 27, 2011. www.castanet.net.

Latimer is a psychiatrist, medical researcher, and writer from British Columbia, Canada.

66 Behavioral and biofeedback therapies can be helpful in teaching an individual with [intermittent explosive disorder] to become aware of the warning signs that may trigger an episode of rage. Cognitive therapy can focus on faulty belief systems and unhealthy thought patterns that trigger anxiety, depression, and anger. 99

—Deborah Bauers, "Intermittent Explosive Disorder: Symptoms and Treatments," Helium, May 25, 2010. www.helium.com.

Bauers is a licensed professional counselor from Monument, Colorado.

66 Even with treatment, it's common to start gambling again (relapse). However, people with pathological gambling can do very well with the right treatment. 99

—National Institutes of Health, "Pathological Gambling," February 18, 2010. www.nlm.nih.gov.

An agency of the US Department of Health and Human Services, the National Institutes of Health is one of the world's leading medical research centers.

Can People Overcome Impulse Control Disorders?

- According to the Mayo Clinic, therapies such as **hypnosis and relaxation techniques** may help reduce the urge to pull hair among trichotillomania sufferers.

- A February 2011 paper by psychiatrists from the Impulse Control Disorders Clinic at the University of Minnesota states that only **65 percent** of people with trichotillomania ever seek treatment.

- According to psychiatrist Daniel A. Plotkin, treatments for pyromania focus primarily on **controlling the disorder** and improving quality of life, rather than on curing the disorder.

- In a 2009 study involving 50 trichotillomania sufferers, **56 percent** significantly reduced their hair pulling after a daily dose of an amino acid known as N-acetylcysteine, compared with **16 percent** of those who were given a placebo.

- The Better Tomorrow Treatment Center in Southern California states that treatment is successful in **95 percent** of children who exhibit signs of pyromania.

- According to psychiatrist Roxanne Dryden-Edwards, about **8 percent** of gamblers who participate in Gamblers Anonymous remain abstinent for one year, and this often improves when they also seek psychotherapy.

A Promising ICD Treatment

People with ICDs are often treated with a combination of therapy and medicine, such as antidepressants. In July 2009 researchers from the University of Minnesota Impulse Control Disorders Clinic published a study in which a group of patients with trichotillomania were treated with an amino acid known as N-acetylcysteine, with the remainder (control group) given a placebo (a harmless substance with no effects). As this graph shows, significant improvement was shown among the N-acetylcysteine group.

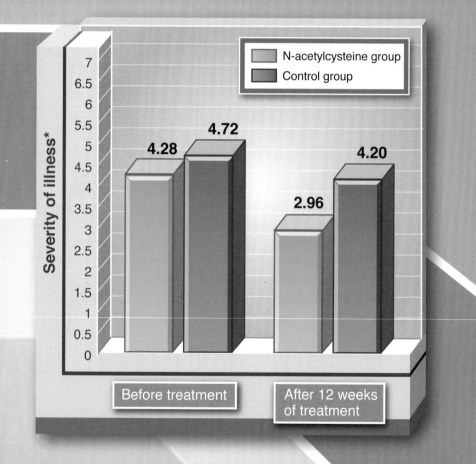

*With 1 being not ill at all, and 7 being the most severe

Source: Jon E. Grant, Brian L. Odlaug, and Suck Won Kim, "N-acetylcysteine, a Glutamate Modulator, in the Treatment of Trichotillomania," *Archives of General Psychiatry*, July 2009. http://archpysc.ama-assn.org.

Embarrassment Biggest Threat to Treatment

In a May 2011 survey by the Shulman Center for Compulsive Theft, Spending & Hoarding, participants were asked why they had not sought treatment for kleptomania, or why they had dropped out after starting treatment.

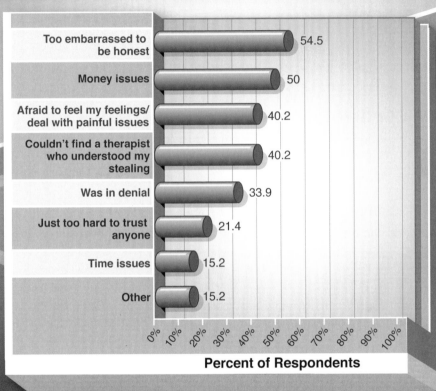

Category	Percent
Too embarrassed to be honest	54.5
Money issues	50
Afraid to feel my feelings/deal with painful issues	40.2
Couldn't find a therapist who understood my stealing	40.2
Was in denial	33.9
Just too hard to trust anyone	21.4
Time issues	15.2
Other	15.2

Percent of Respondents

Note: Participants could choose multiple categories.

Source: Shulman Center for Compulsive Theft, Spending & Hoarding, "Theft/Recovery Survey," May 2011. www.theshulmancenter.com.

- A 2009 study of 100 intermittent explosive disorder patients found that those who took the antidepressant fluoxetine (**Prozac**) for 12 weeks had a significant reduction in their aggressive behavior.

Key People and Advocacy Groups

Elias Aboujaoude: A psychiatrist who directs the Impulse Control Disorders Clinic at Stanford University School of Medicine and is an authority on ICDs.

American Psychiatric Association (APA): The world's largest and most prestigious psychiatric organization.

Arvid Carlsson: A Swedish scientist who was the first to prove that dopamine is one of the brain's neurotransmitters; he eventually was awarded the Nobel Prize for this work.

Jean-Étienne Esquirol: A French psychiatrist who coined the term *monomania* to describe patients who committed impulsive acts even though their minds seemed to be otherwise intact.

Franz Joseph Gall: An eighteenth-century German physician who observed that several prominent men, including an Italian king, habitually stole items for no apparent reason.

Gamblers Anonymous: An organization devoted to helping people recognize and overcome their gambling problems.

Jon E. Grant: A psychiatrist who codirects the Impulse Control Disorders Clinic at the University of Minnesota and who is an expert on ICDs.

Suck Won Kim: A Korean psychiatrist who proposed in 1998 that ICDs were regulated by the same brain circuits as drug addictions. Today he is a researcher with the Department of Psychiatry at the University of Minnesota Medical School.

Emil Kraepelin: A German psychiatrist who wrote about "onioma-niacs," or people who were otherwise ordinary except for uncontrolled shopping and spending behavior.

Charles Chrétian Henry Marc: A French physician who coined the term *monomanie incendiare* ("insane incendiarism") to describe inten-tional fire setters who seemed to be sane individuals despite their heinous crimes.

Brian L. Odlaug: The lead clinical research coordinator for the Impulse Control Disorders Clinic at the University of Minnesota and a noted authority on ICDs.

Isaac Ray: Known as the father of American forensic psychiatry, Ray was among the first to describe disorders of impulse control in an 1838 paper titled "A Treatise on the Medical Jurisprudence of Insanity."

Chronology

1816
Swiss physician Andre Matthey coins the term *klopemanie* to describe thieves who impulsively steal unneeded items, which he attributes to insanity.

1838
In a paper titled "A Treatise on the Medical Jurisprudence of Insanity," psychiatrist Isaac Ray is among the first to write about disorders of impulse control.

1952
Swedish scientist Arvid Carlsson discovers that dopamine is one of the brain's neurotransmitters and that a lack of dopamine in certain areas of the brain could disrupt nerves that control movement.

1800   **1875**   **1950**

1833
French physician Charles Chrétian Henry Marc coins the term *monomanie incendiare* ("insane incendiarism") to describe intentional fire setters who, despite their crimes, seemed to be in full possession of their sanity.

1889
After observing a patient who had pulled out all his body hair, French dermatologist François Henri Hallopeau coins the term *trichotillomania* to describe a disorder that involves the repetitive, irresistible urge to pull one's hair.

1915
In his textbook *Psychiatrie*, German psychiatrist Emil Kraepelin describes an affliction that he calls "oniomania," meaning compulsive buying that leads to serious debt and financial catastrophe.

1904
French psychiatrist Raoul Leroy publishes a paper titled "Pyromania, a Psychosis of Puberty," in which he describes a peculiar mental illness that involves intentional fire setting.

1980
The American Psychiatric Association adds "disorders of impulse control" to the third edition of the DSM.

2011
A study announced by an international team of neuroscientists reveals new information about how the brain controls basic impulses, and could help scientists better understand how ICDs develop.

2010
In a study of 3,090 individuals with Parkinson's disease, 17 percent are found to suffer from at least one ICD, which is attributed to medications that increase dopamine function in the brain.

1980   **1995**   **2010**

1977
Pathological gambling is officially recognized as a psychiatric disorder in the ninth edition of the World Health Organization's *International Classification of Diseases*.

2006
Researchers at Duke University announce their discovery of gene mutations that may be linked to development of trichotillomania.

1998
Korean psychiatrist Suck Won Kim publishes a paper in which he proposes that ICDs are regulated by the same brain circuits as drug addictions.

2000
The fourth edition of the DSM includes diagnostic criteria for kleptomania, pyromania, trichotillomania, intermittent explosive disorder, pathological gambling, and other nonspecific ICDs.

Related Organizations

American Psychiatric Association (APA)

1000 Wilson Blvd., Suite 1825
Arlington, VA 22209
phone: (703) 907-7300; toll-free: (888) 357-7924
e-mail: apa@psych.org • website: www.psych.org

With 36,000 psychiatric physician members, the APA is the world's largest psychiatric organization. Its website provides information about the *Diagnostic and Statistical Manual of Mental Disorders* (DSM), as well as the *Psychiatric News* online magazine, research reports, and a search engine that produces articles about ICDs.

Control Center

9777 Wilshire Blvd., Suite 704
Beverly Hills, CA 90210
phone: (310) 271-8700
e-mail: info@thecontrolcenter.org
website: http://thecontrolcenter.org/impulse.html

Founded by psychiatrist Reef Karim, the Control Center is a treatment facility that specializes in chemical dependency and behavioral addictions. Its website offers a number of articles about ICDs, a link to the *Control Center Blog*, and separate sections that focus on pathological gambling, shopping addiction, sex addiction, and other disorders.

Gamblers Anonymous

International Service Office
PO Box 17173
Los Angeles, CA 90017
phone: (626) 960-3500 • fax: (626) 960-3501
e-mail: isomain@gamblersanonymous.org
website: www.gamblersanonymous.org

Founded in 1957, Gamblers Anonymous is devoted to helping people recognize and overcome their gambling problems. Its website offers an extensive question-and-answer section, information for friends and family members of problem gamblers, an "Are You a Compulsive Gambler?" questionnaire, and numerous publications available for minimal cost.

Impulse Control Disorders Clinic

University of Minnesota, Department of Psychiatry
2450 Riverside Ave.
West Building, 2nd Floor
Minneapolis, MN 55454
phone: (612) 273-8700
e-mail: grant045@umn.edu • website: www.impulsecontroldisorders.org

The Impulse Control Disorders Clinic is devoted to scientific research and patient care. Its website offers numerous articles about ICDs, an illustrated "What Is a Craving?" section, research information, and links to publications by psychiatrists who staff the clinic.

Mayo Clinic

200 First St. SW
Rochester, MN 55905
phone: (507) 284-2511 • fax: (507) 284-0161
website: www.mayoclinic.com

The Mayo Clinic is a world-renowned medical facility that is dedicated to patient care, education, and research. Its website offers comprehensive articles about kleptomania, intermittent explosive disorder, compulsive sexual behavior, and trichotillomania, as well as a number of other articles related to ICDs.

Mental Health America

2000 N. Beauregard St., 6th Floor
Alexandria, VA 22311
phone: (703) 684-7722; toll-free: (800) 969-6642 • fax: (703) 684-5968
e-mail: info@mentalhealthamerica.net
website: www.mentalhealthamerica.net

Mental Health America works to inform, advocate, and enable access to mental health services for all Americans. Its website's search engine produces a number of articles on trichotillomania and other ICDs.

National Center for Responsible Gaming

1299 Pennsylvania Ave. NW, Suite 1175
Washington, DC 20004
phone: (202) 552-2689 • fax: (202) 552-2676
e-mail: info@ncrg.org • website: www.ncrg.org

The National Center for Responsible Gaming is devoted to funding research that helps increase understanding of pathological and youth gambling and find effective methods of treatment. Its website offers news releases, key research findings, the *Wager* online newsletter, and other publications related to problem gambling.

National Council on Problem Gambling (NCPG)

730 Eleventh St. NW, Suite 601
Washington, DC 20001
phone: (202) 547-9204 • fax: (202) 547-9206
e-mail: ncpg@ncpgambling.org • website: www.ncpgambling.org

The NCPG seeks to increase awareness of pathological gambling, ensure the availability of treatment for problem gamblers and their families, and encourage research and prevention programs. Its website offers a vast collection of articles and other resources on problem gambling.

National Institute of Mental Health (NIMH)

Science Writing, Press, and Dissemination Branch
6001 Executive Blvd., Room 8184, MSC 9663
Bethesda, MD 20892
phone: (301) 443-4513; toll-free: (866) 615-6464 • fax: (301) 443-4279
e-mail: nimhinfo@nih.gov • website: www.nimh.nih.gov

The NIMH seeks to reduce mental illness and behavioral disorders through research and supports science that will improve the diagnosis, treatment, and prevention of mental disorders. Numerous articles on ICDs are accessible through the website's search engine.

Shulman Center for Compulsive Theft, Spending & Hoarding

PO Box 250008
Franklin, MI 48025
phone: (248) 358-8508
e-mail: terrenceshulman@theshulmancenter.com
website: www.theshulmancenter.com

Founded by recovered kleptomania sufferer Terrence Shulman, the Shulman Center specializes in treatment for people suffering from kleptomania, compulsive spending, and hoarding. Its website offers personal testimonials, facts and statistics, an online newsletter, videos, and links to other related resources.

Trichotillomania Learning Center (TLC)

207 McPherson St., Suite H
Santa Cruz, CA 95060
phone: (831) 457-1004 • fax: (831) 426-4383
e-mail: info@trich.org • website: www.trich.org

The TLC provides education, outreach, and support of research into the causes and treatments of trichotillomania, skin picking disorder, and related body-focused repetitive behaviors. Its website offers a large collection of articles about these disorders, as well as success stories, research information, and a special section for kids and teenagers.

For Further Research

Books

Elias Aboujaoude and Lorrin M. Koran, eds., *Impulse Control Disorders*. New York: Cambridge University Press, 2010.

Jon E. Grant and Marc N. Potenza, eds., *Oxford Handbook of Impulse Control Disorders*. New York: Oxford University Press, 2012.

Jon E. Grant et al., *Trichotillomania, Skin Picking, and Other Body-Focused Repetitive Behaviors*. Washington, DC: American Psychiatric, 2012.

Angela Hartlin, *Forever Marked: A Dermatillomania Diary*. Raleigh, NC: Lulu, 2010.

Terrence Shulman, *Cluttered Lives, Empty Souls: Compulsive Stealing, Spending & Hoarding*. West Conshohocken, PA: Infinity, 2011.

Mary Sojourner, *She Bets Her Life: A True Story of Gambling Addiction*. Berkeley, CA: Seal, 2010.

Periodicals

Ben Adams, "The Challenges of Arson and Pyromania in Schools," *Fire*, November 2009.

Marcia Angell, "The Epidemic of Mental Illness: Why?," *New York Times Review of Books*, June 23, 2011.

Melinda Beck, "Shop 'til You Stop: How to Treat Compulsive Spending," *Wall Street Journal*, December 6, 2011.

Tom Chiarella, "Pissed Off, On Edge, and Very Tired," *Esquire*, November 2011.

John Cloud, "Sex Addiction: A Disease or a Convenient Excuse?," *Time*, February 28, 2011.

Amanda May Dundas, "I Can't Stop Picking at My Skin. Help!," *Redbook*, January 2011.

Ian Lovett, "Nevada to Cut Funds for Treating Gambling Addiction," *New York Times*, February 19, 2011.

Marie Claire, "The New Addictions," March 2009.

Clayton Simmons, "Manual Manipulation: The Latest 'Psychiatric Bible' Says Who's Sick and Who's Just Fine," *Psychology Today*, May/June 2009.

Katherine Zoepf, "Stealing Beauty," *Allure*, September 2011.

Internet Sources

Jill Denton, "Tiger Woods: Hypersexuality Disorder or Sex Addiction?," *Good Therapy* (blog), March 5, 2010. www.goodtherapy.org/blog/tiger-woods-sex-addiction.

Stephen A. Diamond, "Intermittent Explosive Disorder: No, This Is NOT All About Mel 'Mad Max' Gibson!," *Evil Deeds* (blog), *Psychology Today*, July 15, 2010. www.psychologytoday.com/blog/evil-deeds/201007/intermittent-explosive-disorder-no-is-not-all-about-mel-mad-max-gibson.

Molly Edmonds, "How Trichotillomania Works," Discovery Health, 2012. http://health.howstuffworks.com/skin-care/scalp-care/problems/trichotillomania.htm.

Jeanne M. Fama, "Skin Picking Disorder Fact Sheet," International OCD Foundation, 2010. www.ocfoundation.org/uploadedFiles/MainContent/Find_Help/Skin%20Picking%20Disorder%20Fact%20Sheet.pdf.

Craig Freudenrich, "How Kleptomania Works," Discovery Health, 2012. http://health.howstuffworks.com/mental-health/mental-disorders/kleptomania.htm.

———, "How Pyromania Works," Discovery Health, 2012. http://health.howstuffworks.com/mental-health/mental-disorders/pyromania.htm.

Elizabeth Landau, "Compulsive Shopping: When Spending Is like Substance Abuse," CNN, January 3, 2012. www.cnn.com/2011/12/19/health/mental-health/shopping-addiction-compulsive-buying/index.html.

Fred Penzel and D'Arcy Lyness, reviewers, "Trichotillomania," TeensHealth, May 2009. http://kidshealth.org/teen/your_mind/mental_health/trichotillomania.html.

Samantha Smithstein, "Gains and Losses: Helping People Stop Stealing (Who Can't Stop Themselves)," *What the Wild Things Are* (blog), *Psychology Today*, July 15, 2011. www.psychologytoday.com/blog/what-the-wild-things-are/201107/gains-and-losses-helping-people-stop-stealing-who-cant-stop-the.

Kiera Toffelmire, "Confessions of a Kleptomaniac," *Eyeopener*, October 15, 2010. http://theeyeopener.com/2010/10/confessions-of-a-kleptomaniac.

Source Notes

Overview

1. Pam, "My Name Is Lashes, and I Have Trichotillomania," *Trich-y Business* (blog), March 23, 2008. http://eyelashpuller.blogspot.com.
2. Pam, "My Name Is Lashes, and I Have Trichotillomania."
3. Pam, "That Trichy Feeling," *Trich-y Business* (blog), February 9, 2009. http://eyelashpuller.blogspot.com.
4. Daniel Ploskin, "What Are Impulse Control Disorders?," Psych Central, August 2007. http://psychcentral.com.
5. Quoted in Elias Aboujaoude and Lorrin M. Koran, eds., *Impulse Control Disorders*. New York: Cambridge University Press, 2010, p. 76.
6. Mayo Clinic, "Intermittent Explosive Disorder," June 10, 2010. www.mayoclinic.com.
7. New York University Langone Medical Center, "Self-Mutilation," March 2011. http://psych.med.nyu.edu.
8. Reef Karim, "Sex Addiction or Player?," *Control Center Blog*, February 8, 2010. http://thecontrolcenter.org.
9. Nicole Stelter, "Impulse Control Disorder Symptoms," Livestrong, May 4, 2011. www.livestrong.com.
10. Candice Germain and Michel Lejoyeux, "Pyromania: Clinical Aspects," in Aboujaoude and Koran, *Impulse Control Disorders*, p. 258.
11. Quoted in Susan Maas, "Acting on Impulse," Minnesota Medical Foundation, April 1, 2008. http://blog.lib.umn.edu.
12. Aboujaoude and Koran, *Impulse Control Disorders*, p. xv.
13. Ploskin, "What Are Impulse Control Disorders?"
14. Justin A. Brewer and Marc N. Potenza, "The Neurobiology and Genetics of Impulse Control Disorders: Relationship to Drug Addictions," *Biochemical Pharmacology*, January 1, 2008. www.ncbi.nlm.nih.gov.
15. Ruth Engs, "How Can I Manage Compulsive Shopping and Spending Addiction (Shopoholism)," Indiana University, December 2010. www.indiana.edu.
16. Roxanne Dryden-Edwards, "Gambling Addiction (Compulsive or Pathological Gambling)," MedicineNet, April 7, 2010. www.medicinenet.com.
17. Karim, "Sex Addiction or Player?"
18. Dryden-Edwards, "Gambling Addiction (Compulsive or Pathological Gambling)."

What Are Impulse Control Disorders?

19. Quoted in Maas, "Acting on Impulse."
20. *Lancet*, "Pyromania, a Psychosis of Puberty," March 4, 1905, pp. 583–84.
21. Liana Schreiber, Brian L. Odlaug, and Jon E. Grant, "Impulse Control Disorders: Updated Review of Clinical Characteristics and Pharmacological Management," *Frontiers in Psychiatry*, February 21, 2011. www.frontiersin.org.
22. Germain and Lejoyeux, "Pyromania: Clinical Aspects," in Aboujaoude and Koran, *Impulse Control Disorders*, p. 255.
23. Germain and Lejoyeux, "Pyromania: Clinical Aspects," in Aboujaoude and Koran, *Impulse Control Disorders*, p. 256.
24. Mayo Clinic, "Kleptomania," August 2, 2011. www.mayoclinic.com.
25. Mayo Clinic, "Kleptomania."
26. Quoted in Maas, "Acting on Impulse."
27. Quoted in Sheryl Nance-Nash, "The High Price of America's Gambling

Addiction," *Daily Finance*, July 22, 2011. www.dailyfinance.com.

28. Harvard Medical School, "Treating Intermittent Explosive Disorder," *Harvard Mental Health Letter*, April 2011. www.health.harvard.edu.

29. Stephen A. Diamond, "Intermittent Explosive Disorder: No, This Is NOT All About Mel 'Mad Max' Gibson!," *Evil Deeds* (blog), *Psychology Today*, July 15, 2010. www.psychologytoday.com.

30. Vvacep, comment on Michele R. Berman, "Charlie Sheen, Mel Gibson and Intermittent Explosive Disorder," *Celebrity Diagnosis* (blog), MedPage Today, July 7, 2011. www.medpagetoday.com.

31. Vvacep, comment on Berman, "Charlie Sheen, Mel Gibson and Intermittent Explosive Disorder."

32. Jon E. Grant, *Impulse Control Disorders: A Clinician's Guide to Understanding and Treating Behavioral Addictions*. New York: Norton, 2008, p. 92.

33. Wendy K. Ng and Jose Mejia, "Intrusive Thoughts in a Boy: A Review of Intermittent Explosive Disorder," *McMaster University Medical Journal*, Spring 2011. www.mumj.org.

34. Ng and Mejia, "Intrusive Thoughts in a Boy: A Review of Intermittent Explosive Disorder."

What Causes Impulse Control Disorders?

35. Jon E. Grant, e-mail interview with author, January 29, 2012.

36. *Science Daily*, "Speed of Brain Signals Clocked: New Studies Illuminate Brain's Complex Neurotransmission Machinery," June 22, 2011. www.sciencedaily.com.

37. David A. Nielsen, Dmitri Proudnikov, and Mary Jeanne Kreek, "The Genetics of Impulsivity," in Jon E. Grant and Marc E. Potenza, eds., *Oxford Handbook of Impulse Control Disorders*. New York: Oxford University Press, 2012, p. 225.

38. Quoted in Jean-Claude Dreher and Léon Tremblay, eds., *Handbook of Reward and Decision Making*. Burlington, MA: Academic Press, 2009, p. 293.

39. Samantha Smithstein, "Dopamine: Why It's So Hard to 'Just Say No,'" Pathways Institute for Impulse Control, August 19, 2010. www.pathwaysinstitute.net.

40. Andrew Siderowf, "What Are Impulse Control Disorders in PD Patients and Why Is This Important?," *On the Blog*, National Parkinson Foundation, April 28, 2011. www.parkinson.org.

41. Benjamin James Sadock and Virginia Alcott Sadock, *Synopsis of Psychiatry*. Philadelphia: Lippincott, Williams, & Wilkins, 2007, p. 774.

42. Quoted in Samantha Smithstein, "Gains and Losses: Helping People Stop Stealing (Who Can't Stop Themselves)," *What the Wild Things Are* (blog), *Psychology Today*, July 15, 2011. www.psychologytoday.com.

43. Quoted in Brian Smith, "Cluttered Lives, Empty Souls: Compulsive Stealing, Spending & Hoarding," *Metro Times*, September 28, 2011. http://metrotimes.com.

44. Quoted in Elizabeth Landau, "Compulsive Shopping: When Spending Is like Substance Abuse," CNN, January 3, 2012. www.cnn.com.

45. National Council on Problem Gambling, "FAQ: Problem Gamblers." www.ncpgambling.org.

46. National Council on Problem Gambling, "FAQ: Problem Gamblers."

What Are the Effects of Impulse Control Disorders?

47. Quoted in Kiera Toffelmire, "Confes-

sions of a Kleptomaniac," *Eyeopener*, October 5, 2010. http://theeyeopener .com.

48. Paul Latimer, "Trichotillomania," Castanet, July 27, 2011. www.casta net.net.

49. Maddie M., "Reflections," *TLC Blog*, July 7, 2011. http://blog.trich.org.

50. Maddie M., "Reflections."

51. Jeanne M. Fama, "Skin Picking Disorder Fact Sheet," International OCD Foundation, 2010. www.ocfoundation .org.

52. Quoted in Shannon Kelley, "Skin Picking and Addiction," Fix, May 15, 2011. www.thefix.com.

53. Quoted in Melinda Beck, "Shop 'til You Stop: How to Treat Compulsive Spending," *Wall Street Journal*, December 6, 2011. http://online.wsj .com.

54. Rachel Diaz, "I'm Addicted to Shopping," in *Marie Claire*, "The New Addictions," March 2009, p. 217.

55. Diaz, in *Marie Claire*, "The New Addictions," p. 217.

56. Deborah Bauers, "Intermittent Explosive Disorder: Symptoms and Treatments," Helium, May 25, 2010. www .helium.com.

57. Quoted in Barbara Bradley Hagerty, "Can Your Genes Make You Murder?," WBUR, July 1, 2010. www .wbur.org.

58. Laura M. Letson, "Pathological Gambling: Promoting Risk, Provoking Ruin," in *Impulse Control Disorders,* eds. Elias Aboujaoude and Lorrin M. Koran. New York: Cambridge University Press, 2010, p. 76.

59. Quoted in Nance-Nash, "The High Price of America's Gambling Addiction."

60. Michael J. Burke, "Never Enough," *Michigan Bar Journal*, May 2008. www.michbar.org.

Can People Overcome Impulse Control Disorders?

61. Quoted in Maas, "Acting on Impulse."

62. Quoted in Smithstein, "Gains and Losses."

63. Quoted in Smithstein, "Gains and Losses."

64. Mayo Clinic, "Trichotillomania (Hair-Pulling Disorder)," January 19, 2011. www.mayoclinic.com.

65. Jon E. Grant, Christopher B. Donahue, and Brian L. Odlaug, *Overcoming Impulse Control Problems: A Cognitive-Behavioral Therapy Program*. New York: Oxford University Press, 2011, p. 3.

66. Harvard Medical School, "Treating Intermittent Explosive Disorder."

67. Quoted in Beck, "Shop 'til You Stop."

68. Mayo Clinic, "Depression (Major Depression): Selective Serotonin Reuptake Inhibitors (SSRIs)," December 9, 2010. www.mayoclinic.com.

69. Schreiber et al., "Impulse Control Disorders."

70. Quoted in Maas, "Acting on Impulse."

71. Quoted in Minnesota Medical Foundation, "New University Research Boosts Hopes for People with Impulse Control Disorders," Fall 2009. www .mmf.umn.edu.

72. Jon E. Grant, "N-acetylcysteine for Trichotillomania, Skin Picking, and Nail Biting," Trichotillomania Learning Center, 2009. www.trich.org.

73. Quoted in Deborah Brauser, "Suicide in Gamblers Linked to Increased Psychiatric Disorders, Lower Rates of Help-Seeking," Medscape, December 3, 2010. www.medscape.com.

74. Quoted in CBC News, "Gambling Addict's Suicide a 'Wake-Up Call,'" September 22, 2011. www.cbc.ca.

75. Quoted in Smith, "Cluttered Lives, Empty Souls."

List of Illustrations

Index

Note: Boldface page numbers indicate illustrations.

About the Author

Peggy J. Parks holds a bachelor of science degree from Aquinas College in Grand Rapids, Michigan, where she graduated magna cum laude. An author who has written over 100 educational books for children and young adults, Parks lives in Muskegon, Michigan, a town that she says inspires her writing because of its location on the shores of Lake Michigan.

Lake Zurich MS North
LIBRARY
95 Hubbard Lane
Hawthorn Woods, IL 60047

About the Author

Lake Zurich MS North
LIBRARY
95 Hubbard Lane
Hawthorn Woods, IL 60047